PALAU

PALAU

S E C O N D   E D I T I O N

Nancy Barbour

Full Court Press · San Francisco

Full Court Press
511 Mississippi Street
San Francisco, CA
9 4 1 0 7

Printed in Singapore by Tien Wah Press

Library of Congress Catalog Card Number 95-90296
ISBN: 0-9626344-1-7

This book is provided to the public for the purpose of providing general information about
the Palau Islands. While at the time of publication the information provided to the reader was believed
to be accurate, please be aware that constantly changing economic and ecological conditions on
the islands may result in some information no longer being accurate. Accordingly, the author and publisher
of this book cannot guarantee that the information contained in this book remains
accurate and recommend that the reader check with an island travel bureau to verify hotel accommodations, reef
and weather conditions, or other pertinent information. The information in this book pertaining
to first aid is intended only to provide temporary relief from pain and not as a remedy for any injury.
If injured, you should see a medical professional as soon as possible.

Book Design by Nancy Barbour
Edited by Elaine de Man
Copyedited by Bula Maddison
Text Composition by Phoebe Bixler & Neal Elkin

Photo Credits:
Front Cover by Avi Klapfer
Back Cover:
Clown Triggerfish, Rick Tegeler; Starfish, Ed Robinson; Lionfish, Mitchell P. Warner

CONTENTS

PREFACE

*W*hen I first visited Palau in December of 1986, I fell in love with it. I had never experienced the sheer wonder of diving the Indo-Pacific Ocean, and the islands were some of the most beautiful I had ever seen. After I left, seven short days later, I couldn't stop thinking about Palau. There were so many things I wanted to know, yet little information was readily available. ¶ I returned soon after my first visit with the intention of writing a book about Palau's magnificent reefs so that others, too, could appreciate their rare beauty. But the more I spoke with and got to know the Palauan people, the more intrigued I became with their sacred connection to the surrounding sea — a connection that is revealed in many of their legends. And so the book evolved to include some of these legends in the hope that you, the reader, may also gain some insight into the fascinating culture of Palau — a land whose history, until recently, was not written but passed on from generation to generation through the ancient art of storytelling. ¶ The Palauan people's strong sense of their own heritage and the influence of Western society are apparent to the visitor immediately upon arrival in the islands. Many villages as well as the dive sites have two names, the Palauan name and its English translation. Even the country itself is known by two names, Palau and the more traditional *Belau*. I have chosen to use the name Palau to identify the islands because it is more internationally recognized. In relating the legends, however, I have used the traditional name, *Belau*. ¶ Over the last nine years I have returned to Palau many times and have seen many changes, most notably in the number of tourists who now visit these islands. With this large influx, however, has come a frightening lack of sensitivity to Palau's fragile underwater world. It is my ultimate hope that this book will contribute to your appreciation of Palau and its people, and that, as a result, you will help ensure that Palau remains the unspoiled natural wonder that it is today.

*I*n the most distant past,
there were no people, there was no land. Uchelianged,
the foremost god of heaven, looked down upon this vast
expanse of empty sea and said, "Let there arise a land."
A volcanic rock then rose from the sea and upon it sat
a giant clam. Soon its belly began to swell and tremble,
and it grew larger and larger. But the clam was unable to
give birth. Uchelianged saw this and said, "Let there be a
strong running sea." So the wind began to blow and waves
crashed 'round the clam causing it finally to burst open,
spewing forth swarms of the first sea creatures to swim
the ocean. They in turn gave birth and the once
empty seas were soon teeming with life which was
as much at home on land as in the sea.
And so Belau was born.

In the western Pacific Ocean, beginning just south of Japan, an underwater mountain range known as the Kyushu Ridge extends almost to the shores of New Guinea. Rising to the surface some twenty-seven thousand feet, the tiny exposed peaks of the southernmost mountains form the islands of Palau.

A magnificent barrier reef surrounds most of these islands, creating one of the most spectacular diving areas in the world. The water, nearly as warm as the tropical air, is teeming with fish. Sheer vertical dropoffs start at the ocean's surface and plunge hundreds of feet. Miles and miles of colorful coral reefs abound with exotic marine life. Underwater caves, blue holes, landlocked saltwater lakes and

Preceding pages. The Rock Islands of Palau offer some of the most beautiful scenery in all of Micronesia, and are home to an exotic array of life, both above water and below. First aerial photograph by Neil Montanus. All other Rock Island photographs by Hiroshi Nagano.

Japanese shipwrecks from the Second World War offer a variety of diving rarely found in one area.

Early Palauan legends tell of the richness of these islands and so it is true today. There are more than fourteen hundred species of fish and over seven hundred species of hard and soft coral. By comparison, Hawaii has roughly a third the number of species. Brilliantly colored clownfish nestle among the stinging tentacles of their host anemones. Soft corals grace the reefs with their delicate colors. Manta rays and endangered hawksbill turtles glide through the crystal-clear water. And giant *Tridacna* clams, some over three feet long and more than half a century old, lie in the shallow areas of the inner lagoon. It's no wonder that Palau is considered one of the seven wonders of the underwater world.

There are exotic marine animals in Palau rarely found in other parts of the world. The dugong, a marine mammal reduced to near extinction elsewhere, has managed to survive partly because ancient traditional law allowed the taking of dugongs only for Palauans of the highest rank. And rare saltwater crocodiles live in the mangrove swamps around the big island of Babeldaob as well as in some of the marine lakes within the famous Rock Islands.

Palau is the only island group in Micronesia where crocodiles are found. They are not, however, seen on the offshore reefs where most of the dive sites are located. But sharks are a common sight — whitetips, blacktips and grey reef sharks are the species most often encountered. Fortunately, they are not a threat to divers, for the surrounding waters offer an abundance of food. Typically un-aggressive, these sharks are far more fascinating than frightening.

In addition to exciting marine life, intriguing shipwrecks await exploration. More than sixty Japanese ships were destroyed in Palau during the Second World War. Although many of these ships have been salvaged, there are diveable wrecks that equal those of the famous Chuuk (Truk) Lagoon. And there are sunken ships that have yet to be found. One of the few American ships known to have sunk in Palau is believed to be lying in just one hundred feet of water off the southern shores of the island of Angaur, and rumors persist of a sunken Japanese hospital ship laden with a secret cargo of gold.

Not only are Palau's reefs teeming with life, but her islands are home to a variety of land animals as well. Colorful parrots fly high over the Rock Islands, along with sulphur-crested cockatoos and Micronesian fruit bats. The Palauan owl, secretive by nature and rarely seen in the wild, lives deep in the heart of the tropical forest where the haunting calls of the Palauan fruit dove echo through the trees. Ferns and delicate orchids grow among the dense jungle foliage where at sundown a chorus of crickets, tiny tree frogs and sly geckos fill the warm night air. Giant coconut crabs forage through the jungle as well as monitor lizards that can be three feet long. And a pack of wild macaque monkeys, the only monkeys found in Micronesia, thrives on the southern island of Angaur.

Palau's vast natural wealth is equaled by a culture rich in heritage and oral tradition — ancient wisdom that has been passed from generation to generation through chants, myths and colorful legends. From these legends, a number of which appear among these pages, much can be learned about the mysteries of these islands and their people.

*S*oon *after the creation of
the world, there was only one island. And on this island,
which they called Angaur, there lived a child born of a
goddess from the sea. The child's name was Chuab and she
was possessed of a voracious appetite. She ate so much and
grew into such an enormous giant that the people became
threatened with famine. One night while she slept, they tied
her up and set her ablaze. Chuab roared and kicked and
Angaur shook. The struggle was so fierce that Chuab kicked
herself into many pieces, large and small, which settled
upon the ocean and formed the islands of Belau.*

Palau is an elongated chain of more than three hundred islands
that stretch across four hundred miles of ocean in a north-south direction. Only
eight of the islands are inhabited. The population is a mere fifteen thousand, the
majority of whom live in the capital city of Koror. Most of Palau's 188 square
miles of land is concentrated in a central cluster of islands that extends from the
atolls of Kayangel in the north to Angaur in the south. Two hundred miles farther
south and stretching across yet another two hundred miles of ocean toward New
Guinea are the six, small, isolated coral islands often referred to as the Southwest
Islands. Though these islands are technically a part of Palau, the inhabitants,

*Over the centuries, the Rock Islands have been transformed into distinctive shapes, so undercut at
their bases that from a distance they appear to be floating above the water's surface. This erosion is
believed to be due to a combination of physical, chemical and biological processes. As rain water
slowly seeps down through the rotting vegetation on the limestone island, it becomes acidic. In calm
weather this acidic water forms a floating lens that surrounds the island and slowly eats away its
limestone base. Further damage is caused by marine organisms such as sea urchins, chitons and
limpets, which graze on the algae growing between the tidemarks on the limestone base.*

all eighty of them, speak a dialect more similar to that of the neighboring Caroline Islands.

Palau is famous for its breathtaking coral reefs, but the scenery above water is just as spectacular. The island geology is unique, for rarely do you find such diverse formations in such close proximity. The volcanic island of Babel-daob, the second largest island in Micronesia, rises more than seven hundred feet above sea level and hosts inland waterfalls surrounded by lush tropical rain forests. In contrast, the four low-lying islands of Kayangel sit atop a limestone reef growing from the rim of a submerged volcano, creating an exquisite coral atoll that rises but a few feet above sea level. With deserted white sand beaches and a shallow turquoise lagoon, Kayangel fits the classic Western image of a tropical island paradise.

The southern islands of Peleliu and Angaur are broad reef flats that were thrust above sea level by volcanic forces. Deep caves and natural crevices now riddle the land. During World War II, Japanese soldiers used the caves on the island of Peleliu to construct an intricate system of passages and underground fortifications that were undetected by American aerial reconnaissance. The Americans mistakenly thought the island could be easily taken, but the invasion turned into one of the bloodiest of the Pacific war. More than two thousand tons of explosives were spent before the American flag flew over Peleliu.

But the most fascinating geological formations in Palau are the Rock Islands — the scenic highlight of all Micronesia. These islands, scattered throughout the central and southern part of the Palauan archipelago, are the remains of ancient coral reefs uplifted by volcanic forces millions of years ago. Some tower hundreds of feet above the ocean and are covered with dense tropical jungle, others are barely large enough to support a single coconut tree. All have been undercut at the water-line by centuries of erosion and algae-eating marine organisms, giving them the appearance of giant emerald mushrooms. Secluded sand beaches backed by nearly impenetrable jungle fringe the shores of many of these uninhabited islands.

Hidden within the interiors of some of the larger Rock Islands are mysterious saltwater lakes, many connected to the surrounding ocean by underground tunnels that range in size from small fissures to openings large enough to swim through. Palau is home to more of these marine lakes — over seventy — than anywhere else in the world. These lakes vary not only in size, but in temperature, salinity and inhabitants as well. The water temperature in one lake is more than a hundred degrees just fifteen feet below the surface. Another lake is populated almost entirely by a species of jellyfish found nowhere else, and still another supports a complete tropical reef community including sharks and an occasional transient saltwater crocodile.

One tightly clustered, isolated group of Rock Islands known as the Seventy Islands was designated a wildlife preserve by the Palauan government in 1956. Today it is a well-known nesting ground for the hawksbill turtle and the rare Micronesian megapode — a gull-sized, ground-dwelling bird that lays eggs in a huge mound of soil sometimes as large as fifteen feet across. The Seventy Islands form a protected environment for much of Palau's wildlife, and by law no one is allowed on the islands.

Though the scenery of Palau is as beautiful as it is diverse, the islands themselves are filled with mystery and intrigue. Angered spirits of the ancestral dead are thought to roam through the islands at night. Giant stone faces, their origins unknown, lie scattered throughout the large island of Babeldaob. Ancient rock paintings adorn the near inaccessible cliffs of Ulong Island. And the mysterious stone monoliths of Badrulchau stand in mute testimony to a prehistoric civilization of which little is known.

*W*hen the giant child
*Chuab fell into the sea, she came to rest on her side,
facing the western sky. The great bulk of her body became the
island of Babeldaob — her back forming the east coast, her
front becoming the western shore. And this fertile new land
became home for the people. Chuab's head rested in the village
of Ngerchelong, and for this reason the people there are smart.
Her shoulders became the village of Ngaraard, and here
the people are strong. Her stomach came to lie in the village
of Ngiwal, and that is why the people there eat seven times
a day. Her legs became the islands of Peleliu and Angaur,
where the people are known for their fleetness. And Chuab's
private parts came to rest in the village of Aimeliik,
where, it is said, the rain always begins.*

Though the origin of the Palauan people is shrouded in folkfore
and legend, the most accepted theory, based on linguistic similarities, holds that
the islands were settled thousands of years ago by people migrating from northern
Indonesia, the Philippines and Melanesia — people who thought nothing of
sailing hundreds of miles across uncharted seas in open outrigger canoes.

The early Palauans were perhaps once gifted navigators, but when they
got to Palau they stayed. With an abundance of food from the fertile land and

---

*Many traditional customs are still practiced today in Palau, including a ceremony popularly
known as* ngasech, *the celebration of the first-born child. After the birth of her baby, the
new mother undergoes a series of medicinal steam baths,* omesurech, *lasting from several days
to more than a week, depending on the rank of her clan. On the last day of the bathing, she
is anointed with turmeric and coconut oil, dressed in traditional clothes and presented,* mo
tuobed, *to her family and friends. In the ensuing celebration, the women guests sing chants
and dance around the new mother. Afterwards, an elaborate feast is served.*

surrounding reefs, there was no need to explore beyond their shores. Long distance navigation skills diminished. Instead, the men became great fishermen and knew more about the seasonal rhythms and life cycles of fish than is known by Western scientists even today. While the sea was essentially the men's domain, farming the land was where the women excelled, primarily growing taro, a staple food with tuberous roots that are cooked in a variety of ways. The labor of the women guaranteed an adequate supply of food year round and thus gave them high social and political importance in the community.

The men, freed from the time-consuming and physically demanding task of farming, devoted their energies to other village affairs, primarily the construction of public buildings, canoe houses and elaborate stone causeways, docks and tree-lined stone paths. Politics was foremost on the minds of most men as was inter-village warfare. Competition was, and still is, a highly motivating force between individuals, clans, villages and states. Historically there was a great power struggle between the north and the south, a rivalry that continues to this day.

The arts flourished. Women were fine weavers and wove intricate baskets, blankets and sails for canoes. The men worked with wood and carved elaborate bowls, plates and large, intricate food containers that were inlaid with shell. Master craftsmen built great war canoes nearly sixty feet long and sleek sailing canoes as long as thirty-three feet with a beam of a mere fourteen inches. Though these canoes were considered some of the finest in all of Micronesia, the most outstanding example of Palauan craftsmanship was the *bai*, a gathering place for the men of the village. The *bai* was a masterpiece of Micronesian architecture. Built with large, heavy planks from trees that were felled and carved without the benefit of metal tools, the high-peaked structure was held together by nothing more than the precise fit of the wooden beams, then lashed together with coconut sennit rope. The most elaborately constructed *bai* functioned as a meeting place or council house for the governing chiefs of the village. Other *bai* served as clubhouses — gathering places for the men of the village where the traditional skills of fishing, hunting, building and warfare were learned. The interior beams and outside gables of each *bai* were decorated with carved and painted stories depicting historic events of the village, humorous tales and legends of importance to the community.

The early Palauans developed a complex and highly organized social system that today mystifies all but the most dedicated anthropologist. In the Palauan matrilineal system, which still exists, nuclear families and extended families, called clans, were related through the mother's side of the family. The mother's brother had a role nearly equal to that of the natural father in providing for the children. And many children were adopted, always within the extended family and often as a means to manipulate land, wealth and human resources. Men ruled as chiefs, but it was the women who chose those chiefs and had the power to rescind chiefly status. Women also held the money of the clan.

Money made from beads of colored glass or high-fired clay, substances not known to exist in Palau, was used in a complex system of exchange. Each piece was named, its previous clan owners known and its specific shape, as individual as a fingerprint, committed to memory in the minds of certain elders. Even today, much of a clan's history can be told through its money. This money continues to be used in certain traditional marriage, funeral and first-child ceremonies though, as it was in the past, it is the responsibility of the recipient to verify its authenticity.

As a result of more than a century of foreign influence, and more recently in an effort to meet the needs of a developing nation, many aspects of the traditional culture have changed. The outboard motor has replaced the outrigger canoe, much of the ancient fishing knowledge is on the verge of being lost and men now gather in restaurants instead of the *bai* to discuss the politics of their world. As nearly half of the work force is employed by the government, the dollar now reigns over a once-subsistence economy. Today, few young women are willing to work in the taro patches — the gardens are now tended mostly by female elders of the village. And though hereditary chiefs continue to influence political decisions, their traditional authority is often in conflict with the elected·officials of the current Western-style democratic government.

Yet even though the people of Palau are very cosmopolitan, well-educated and Western in appearance, many traditions remain. Most, however, involve a complex system of social obligations not seen by the casual observer. One aspect of the culture that is quite apparent is the friendly and gregarious nature of the people, many of whom continue the time-honored custom of chewing betel nut, a green palm nut sprinkled with powdered lime and wrapped in a leaf from a pepper tree. When chewed, this concoction turns the saliva red, and over time the smiles of the elderly become bright red slashes.

In addition many of the older customs and art forms that had been slowly dying are seeing a rebirth. New *bai*, built in the traditional style, have recently been constructed in several villages, and traditional sailing canoes are again being built by the elders in Koror. The ancient carvings that appeared on the *bai* have evolved into storyboards, carved pieces of wood depicting colorful Palauan legends, which have become the most well-known art form in the country today. In the northern villages of Kayangel and Ngerchelong, the chiefs have reinstated an age-old conservation law known as *bul*, which prohibits fishing on certain reefs during critical spawning periods. And Palauan dance experts throughout the islands still teach their children the traditional songs and dances, and on special occasions one can see young people adorned with flowers and shell jewelry perform in the traditional dress of their cultural ancestors.

Both public and family celebrations commonly involve traditional aspects of Palauan culture. Clothing made of locally grown materials, in a manner passed down through generations, is proudly worn on these occasions. These photographs, taken during various public celebrations, provide colorful examples of traditional Palauan dress.

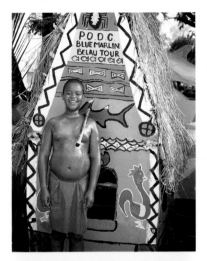

*L*ong ago there was a great
navigator from the small island of Yap who braved the
long ocean journey to Belau in an outrigger canoe. There,
among the limestone caves of the Rock Islands, he found a
sparkling stone that was unlike anything he had ever seen.
At first he cut a piece of the stone in the shape of a fish.
But he was not satisfied. He then cut the stone in the shape of
a crescent moon. But he was still not satisfied. Finally, he
settled on a piece shaped like a full moon and cut a hole in its
center so the enormous stone could be carried on a pole and
loaded onto his canoe. He then sailed back across the sea with
his newly found treasure, the first stone money in Yap.

By the end of the seventeenth century, after more than two
hundred years of European exploration of the Pacific, Spain had laid claim to
much of Micronesia. But the Spaniards knew little, if anything, of the islands of
Palau. Finally, in 1710, Spanish captain Don Francisco de Padilla landed his ship
Santissima Trinidad in the Palau Islands. As so often happens when two different
cultures meet for the first time, confusion erupted when the Palauans thought
they were rightfully entitled to all of the ship's movable pieces of iron. Shots were
fired by the Spanish only to be returned by a volley of spears from the Palauans.
Padilla quickly weighed anchor and left.

Although the islands of Palau remained virtually unknown to the Western world during the first
two centuries of European exploration of the Pacific, the people of Yap knew exactly where Palau
was. They routinely made the five-hundred-mile round-trip journey to Palau in outrigger canoes,
navigating by the stars. Once in Palau, they quarried enormous pieces of stone money. This money,
the largest in the world, often measured ten to twelve feet in diameter and was carved from the
crystalline limestone of Palau's Rock Islands. Photograph courtesy of the Belau National Museum

It wasn't until seventy-five years later that any significant contact between Europeans and Palauans took place and this happened solely by accident. On the night of August 10, 1783, in storm-tossed seas, the British captain Henry Wilson wrecked his ship, the *Antelope*, on the western reefs of Palau. Wilson and his crew were able to salvage some supplies and row to the nearby uninhabited island of Ulong, where they spent three months rebuilding their ship with the help and support of Chief Ibedul of Koror. Such a strong friendship developed between the two leaders that on the day of Wilson's departure the British captain was honored with the highest distinction in Palau — a bracelet made from the vertebrae of a dugong was ceremonially placed on his wrist. In appreciation Wilson gave the Ibedul guns, gifts that would have a great impact upon the subsequent balance of power among the villages of Palau.

The favorable reports of Wilson's experiences helped open the islands to further foreign contact. Over the next hundred years Palau saw an influx of British traders, American whalers and German merchants who introduced, among other things, deadly contagious diseases. By the 1900s, Palau's population had dropped from forty thousand to less than four thousand. The presence of these British and German "foreigners" also threatened Spain's hold on the islands. In 1885 Pope Leo XIII upheld Spain's three-hundred-year-old claim to Micronesia — a claim that persisted until the Spanish-American War, which marked the end of Spain as a Pacific power. In 1899 Spain sold Palau to Germany.

Germany's main interest in Palau was economic. Phosphate, a valuable fertilizer, was mined on the southern island of Angaur. In addition, coconut plantations were set up throughout the islands to expand Germany's profitable trade in copra, the dried meat of the coconut from which oil is extracted.

Germany's control of Palau lasted only fifteen years. Japan seized the islands in 1914, at the beginning of World War I, and remained in power for the next thirty years. Japan expanded the commercial ventures started by the Germans and built a thriving economy based on phosphate and bauxite mining, commercial fishing, and the farming of rice, pineapples and coconuts.

Koror became the administrative center for Japan's Pacific island empire. Japanese citizens were encouraged to emigrate to Palau, and they soon outnumbered the Palauans four to one. It was during this period that the Palauan culture saw its most dramatic change. There was a shift in power from village chiefs to Japanese administrators and Koror became a stylish Asian metropolis with public baths, gourmet restaurants and geishas. During the 1930s Japan began fortifying the islands as an imperial outpost and by 1938 Palau was a closed military area.

In 1944, in the throes of World War II, American forces determined that Palau was a logical stepping-stone in their push toward the Philippines and, ultimately, Japan. Their main target was the airfield on the island of Peleliu. The Americans thought the island was flat and could be easily taken. In reality, the land was composed of elevated limestone ridges riddled with natural caves that had been heavily fortified by the Japanese. When American forces stormed the island on September 15th, they were faced with mountainous peaks rising over two hundred feet, ground of jagged coral rocks sharp enough to cut through the soles of shoes, and an enemy ready and willing to fight until death. The battle lasted nearly three months. At one point American forces controlled the surface, but the entrenched Japanese were literally underneath their feet and there was no way to dislodge them. The battle at Peleliu was one of the toughest, bloodiest operations of the Pacific war. An estimated eleven thousand Japanese and one thousand Americans lost their lives.

World War II shattered Palau. Caught in the cross-fire between Japanese and American forces, Palauans were the victims of events over which they had no control. Food was in short supply, medical care was minimal, schools were closed, trade was ruined. As a result, traditional Palauan authority began to re-emerge. At the end of World War II, the United States took control of a physically destroyed nation and a people eager for self-government.

In 1947, Palau, as well as the Caroline, Marshall and Marianas Islands (with the exception of Guam), became a trust territory of the United Nations, administered by the U.S. government. Known as the Trust Territory of the Pacific Islands, the area was designated as a Strategic Trust, which gave the United States the right to establish military bases on the islands. As the administrating authority, the United States had the responsibility to oversee the development of the islands until the islanders were ready to choose either independence or continued political ties. The Trust Territory was eventually divided into four political districts, the Republic of Palau being one of them. By the mid-1980s, three of the four territories had negotiated agreements with the United States concerning their political status. Palau, however, after electing its first president in 1980, adopted the world's first nuclear-free constitution, a constitution that was at odds with the U.S. intentions of transiting nuclear materials through Palauan territory. It took another thirteen years of negotiations, ten votes by the Palauan people and an amendment to the constitution — during which time the first president of the country was assassinated and the second president died from a gunshot wound to the head — before an agreement between the two governments was reached.

Under the terms of the agreement, known as the Compact of Free Association, the United States was granted certain airfield and harbor rights in the islands for the next fifty years. In return Palau receives, among other things, nearly $450 million over a fifteen-year period. On October 1, 1994, the people of Palau raised their national flag over their young island nation and welcomed in a new era of political sovereignty.

The bai, *an elaborately decorated building where the village Council of Chiefs would meet, was the central focus of each village in traditional times. Photograph courtesy of the Belau National Museum*

*T*he maximum speed limit on the streets of Palau is a leisurely twenty-five miles per hour. Palauans make up for this when they get behind the wheel of a boat. Most of the local speedboats are equipped with powerful twin outboard motors and can really move. Even so, the dive sites are anywhere from twenty minutes to an hour from Koror, but the scenery along the way is spectacular and time passes quickly.

Most of Palau's dive sites are located along the outer edge of the barrier reef, with the most popular ones concentrated in the southwestern corner. Dive operators typically offer day-long excursions with two tank dives. Boats leave the docks around 9:00 A.M. and return between 3:30 and 5:00 P.M. There is a two-hour lunch break between dives which provides ample time for relaxing on a sun-drenched beach, snorkeling along a shallow reef, or just sitting on the boat and gazing out to sea. The return trip to Koror often passes through the beautiful Rock Islands, the uninhabited, complex maze of islands for which Palau has become famous. Zooming through shallow lagoons with the wind in your hair and the coral inches below your feet, and passing within a whisper of an undercut limestone island, is an adventure in itself and an exciting way to end an exciting day of diving.

Palau is famous for its spectacular vertical walls that drop hundreds of feet yet grow to within several feet of the surface. Many consider the coral reefs of Palau to be among the most beautiful in the world — assets that have not gone

Preceding page. Some of the most spectacular dropoffs in Palau are located around the Ngemelis Islands along the southwestern barrier reef. This area is known for its sheer vertical walls that drop nearly one thousand feet and the shallow reef tops that grow to within several feet of the surface. Photograph by Mitchell P. Warner

unnoticed. Where there were only three dive operators a short time ago, now there are more than twenty, many of whom cater primarily to divers from Japan. With the growing number of dive operators has come a variety of diving styles — ranging from divers being responsible for their own depth, bottom time and safety to the practice of diving in a group. There are dive guides on every boat, but some stay with the group, some don't. Predive briefings run the gamut as well, from detailed descriptions of the reef and local marine life to simply, "Keep the wall on your right."

Whatever style of diving you prefer, be aware that the clear water and near-vertical dropoffs make deep dives tempting. At the time of this writing, not all of the dive boats carry oxygen, crucial during the first critical moments in the treatment of a diving accident. And even though there is a recompression chamber at the hospital in Koror, it's a lousy way to spend an afternoon.

Most diving in Palau is drift diving — the current carries you along the edge of the reef and the boat picks you up wherever you finally surface. Although you generally drift along at a leisurely pace, there are a few dive sites where strong currents are possible — notably Blue Corner, Peleliu Corner and New Dropoff. Not surprisingly, these are also the most popular dives because strong currents mean lots of fish. Sailing along a beautiful coral dropoff surrounded by enormous schools of pelagic fish is what diving in Palau is all about.

Because of the currents, deep vertical dropoffs and possible minimal supervision, the dive sites along the outer barrier reef are recommended for inter-mediate to advanced divers. However, no matter what your level of experience, all dive boats go to the most popular sites, so if you are uncomfortable in currents, let your dive operator know that you would prefer to dive reefs that are not as challenging. Even if you are not a scuba diver, many beautiful areas around the Rock Islands offer superb snorkeling. A delicate field of soft coral, one of the larger concentrations of these corals in Palau, grows in just twenty feet of water in a natural arch between two Rock Islands. A Japanese zero lies in ten feet of water on the eastern side of Palau, and more than a hundred giant *Tridacna* clams —

some over three feet long and weighing several hundred pounds — grow in the shallow waters just offshore of a beautiful Rock Island beach. You can also arrange a snorkeling trip to famous Jellyfish Lake.

You can request any type of diving you want, within reason and for a price. Perhaps you would rather make three dives a day instead of the usual two or dive once in the morning and spend the afternoon on a secluded beach. Maybe you would like to explore the pristine reefs of the southernmost island of Angaur or fly to the beautiful northern atoll of Kayangel by float plane and dive in areas that few others have seen. You can even charter a private sailboat and dive and snorkel to your heart's content. These arrangements and more can be made with the local dive or tour operators. Travel agents in the United States who specialize in diving can also arrange week-long or ten-day cruises on board one of the several live-aboard dive boats.

No matter what time of the year you visit Palau, there are always places to dive because of the variety of locations around the islands. However, your best chance for clear skies and calm weather is from late December to June — there are fewer chances of heavy rain showers and winds are less likely to affect the more popular dive sites along the southwestern barrier reef. During the late summer months, days of exceptionally calm water and glorious sunshine alternate with days of heavy rains. Typhoons, however, are rare. In years when normal weather patterns prevail, the driest months are generally February, March and April — the wettest, June, July and August. But with more than 150 inches of rain annually, you can expect showers at any time. As one Palauan boat driver explains, "During our dry season, it rains a little bit less than our rainy season."

Water temperatures remain constant throughout the year, averaging 82 to 84 degrees. Visibility ranges from 50 to over 100 feet along the outer barrier reef and is greatly influenced by the weather and daily tides. The tides not only play a crucial role in the visibility but also in the types of marine life you will encounter. As a general rule, the water is clearest along the outer barrier reef on an incoming tide and the reefs are swarming with fish. On an outgoing tide, visibility is reduced and schools of fish are not as abundant, giving you a chance to focus on the dazzling variety of corals and tropical fish. The dive sites are different every day and every time you dive them. You can dive a reef at high tide and return just an hour later and your dive will be completely different. Dive operators make every effort to select the best dive sites to take advantage of changing tide conditions. Trust your dive guide — if he or she says it is too rough to dive a certain site, it's too rough to dive that site.

Dive boats range from open outboard-powered skiffs to larger cabin cruisers. Though most of the boats have shade canopies, some don't, so bring sun protection — Palau is only 7 degrees north of the equator and the sun is intense. You will also want to bring diving booties, zoris or some other type of rubber-soled shoes for walking from the boat to the beach during the midday lunch break. And a lightweight nylon windbreaker will provide warm, welcome relief when it rains.

Most of the local dive shops offer rental equipment and several sell top-of-the-line gear, but if you are coming to Palau to dive, it makes more sense to bring your own equipment — mask, fins, regulator, depth and pressure gauge and a BC, equipment that fits and that you're familiar with. And even in these warm waters most divers prefer to wear a lightweight wetsuit or Lycra bodysuit. It is also a good idea to bring an inflatable safety sausage to help the boat operators find you when you surface at the end of a dive. Although local boat drivers pride themselves on being able to locate divers in the water, when the weather is rough it never hurts to help them out. It is also recommended that you bring a pocket signal strobe and a Dive Alert horn. Dive operators provide tanks, weights and belts.

Film and batteries are available in Koror, but if you have a favorite film or your camera uses an unusual battery, bring them with you. There are several 24-hour print film developers in town, and E-6 processing for slide film is now available. There are also several shops that will repair underwater cameras.

Palau has justifiably gained a reputation as one of the best diving destinations in the world. Although most of the popular dive sites have similar profiles — dropoffs that are deep, steep and swarming with fish — each of Palau's reefs has its own personality. The following pages will attempt to give you an idea of what to expect at some of the more popular dive sites, but nothing compares with being there.

You don't have to be a diver to enjoy Palau's beautiful marine life. Here at Soft Coral Arch, hundreds of pastel colored soft corals live in a natural arch between two Rock Islands. Growing from a depth of twenty feet, this beautiful garden of coral reaches nearly to the surface. And just off the shore of Neco Island, there is a shallow reef full of corals and colorful tropical fish. Nearby, more than a hundred giant clams live in just ten to thirty feet of water, and several Japanese seaplanes from the Second World War lie in a shallow cove within minutes of Koror by boat. Photograph by Hiroshi Nagano

*T*here once was a
*fisherman who set his traps in an area of the reef
that was unfamiliar to him. To find his traps, he had
to triangulate their locations. But instead of marking
the new locations from land he used the clouds,
and he never found his fish traps again.*

Siaes (See-eye-es) Tunnel is located along a remote section of
Palau's western barrier reef. In what seems like the middle of nowhere, with few
landmarks in sight, dive guides somehow manage to anchor right over the tunnel.
The amazing thing is that Siaes Tunnel was discovered by accident. Back in the
early 1980s a group of divers was on the way to Siaes Corner, located a little
farther north and a beautiful dive in its own right. The pace of the islands being
what it is, the local dive guide didn't feel up to going the extra distance and
instead dropped his group along an unexplored area of the reef. As they descended
the vertical wall, they discovered the enormous tunnel 100 feet below.

Although called a tunnel, Siaes is more like a hugh swim-through cave with
openings at either end and a third midway through. Enough natural light filters
into the cavern to make the dive without a light, but if you have one, bring it —
the colorful sponges and corals that encrust the walls of the cave come alive. This
is a deep dive. The ceiling lies at 80 feet and the bottom at nearly 130, so be

Soft corals, Dendronephthya *sp., are among the most beautiful of all corals. These animals
are often found in areas exposed to currents where they can capture drifting planktonic prey.
Some species of soft coral inflate their bodies with water to maximize their ability to feed in the
nutrient-rich tidal flow. When the current slows, the animals deflate and await the rhythmic
flow of water to begin again. Photograph by Ed Robinson*

prepared for a dive of 90 to 100 feet even if you stay near the ceiling. At these depths, there never seems to be enough time to fully explore the cavern inside, but with so much to see, it is fun to stay as long as you can. Ancient bushes of black coral grow from the ceiling and inside walls of the cave. A large stingray occasionally lies buried on the sandy floor of the cavern or a rare pantherfish quietly swims among the coral. At the opposite end of the tunnel, there is an archway framed by seven-foot sea fans softly backlit from the outside light. Exploring the inside of this deep, dark cavern is as thrilling as it is beautiful.

The small window exit midway through the tunnel is one of the most peaceful places on the reef. Surrounded by a garden of small sea fans and soft corals, it is a beautiful area to take photographs or just gaze out into the 600 miles of open ocean that stretches before you. Grey reef sharks often cruise along the outer wall, and at times you may even see the silhouette of a graceful manta ray in the distance. Siaes Reef forms the northern tip of a huge underwater bay that juts far out into the prevailing currents of the Philippine Sea so you might even see large pelagic fish such as wahoo, tuna and on rare occasions even marlin.

Because of its depth, Siaes Tunnel is recommended for experienced divers. If you don't feel like exploring the deep tunnel, the surrounding reef, which reaches to within 20 feet of the surface, offers plenty to see. Schools of spectacular square-spot anthias weave among the corals along with hundreds of pyramid butterflys, a brightly colored yellow, black and white fish common along the outer reefs of Palau. If you're lucky, you might even see a leopard shark, a harmless species similar in appearance to the nurse shark but unique to the Indo-Pacific. On occasion they lie in the sandy areas along this reef, sometimes as shallow as 60 feet, although they seem to prefer the deeper areas between 100 and 130 feet.

A tiny hermit crab, Paguristes *sp. barely half an inch long, peers out from the safety of its coral burrow. Photograph by Hiroshi Nagano*

*Oreng, the most beautiful
young girl in all of Belau, was in love with a poor
boy from another village. But Osilek, the chief of Ulong
Island, was determined to have her for his bride instead.
Osilek had many canoes and the biggest fishnet in all of
Belau. His wealth would bring good fortune to the family.
Oreng had no choice but to marry the old chief, and soon
afterward her young lover died of a broken heart. Oreng fled to
his side upon hearing this news, and when she saw her dear
lover she lay down beside him. And there in her sorrow she too
died. Osilek was standing high upon a cliff when he learned
what had happened. Angrily, he stomped his foot so hard that
he lost his balance and fell into the sea. There he turned to
stone and to this day the stone can still be seen. It is said
that a certain butterfly now lives on Ulong Island, one
that always flies in threes — two together, the third
following. The trio is believed to be Oreng at last
with her lover and Osilek chasing close behind.*

Ulong (Oo-long) Channel is a special place. Not only is the coral here some of the most beautiful you will ever see, but this channel is one of the largest grouper breeding grounds in Palau. During the full moons of May, June and July hundreds of these fish gather here to breed. This natural channel, which cuts only partway through the western barrier reef, is best seen on an incoming tide when the water is clear and the current strong. But the tides here are so

One of the many highlights of Ulong Channel is this beautiful chalice coral, Turbinaria.
*Its immense size suggests it could be more than several hundred years old. Among its many
residents is an anemone,* Heteractis magnifica, *with a resident of its own, a pinkfaced
clownfish,* Amphiprion perideraion. *Photograph by Kevin Davidson*

fluky, even the pros don't always get it right. Sometimes you drift into the channel only to find yourself struggling against the current halfway through.

A steep wall fronts the mouth of the channel where huge grouper lurk in the deeper water over 100 feet. Mantas occasionally pass by this dropoff, and at times a roving pack of juvenile grey reef sharks storms past the coral. A school of batfish often hugs the corner of the reef just as you turn toward the mouth of the channel, where grey reef sharks circle through schools of jacks and small barracuda that gather to feed on an incoming tide.

Once you drift into the channel itself, mountains of hard coral line its sloping sides along with delicate soft corals, leather corals and more — you won't see prettier coral. And rarely will you find such variety. Scientists have counted more than 90 species of coral just in this channel alone. Depth of the channel ranges from 35 to 50 feet, where rainbow-colored parrots, elegant fire gobies and blackspotted puffers thrive. Goupers are seen here throughout the year, but during the summer months several of the larger species gather in the channel to breed. And these fish are big, two to three feet long, but difficult to see as they nervously duck into small cracks in the coral only to disappear into the maze of passages that wind through the reef. Because this is such a sensitive breeding area, fishing is prohibited here from April through July. There is even talk of closing the channel to divers during this critical spawning season.

One area about midway through the channel is a favorite haunt for nesting triggerfish, pound for pound the most aggressive fish on the reef. Although barely over a foot long, these fish don't think twice about charging something six times their size, such as you. They rarely charge unless provoked, but when tending a nest they don't want anything anywhere near them. If you see them blowing into the sand on the floor of the channel, assume they have a nest and give them wide berth or they'll rocket from the bottom with you in their sights. At times as many as 15 nests lie in this one area alone and it feels like you're dodging stray bullets — big ones with teeth. If you stay shallow and to the sides of the channel when drifting through this area, the triggerfish will generally leave you alone.

One of the highlights of this dive is the enormous chalice coral that lies near the far end of the channel — its wafer-thin plates stacked one upon the other forming countless cracks and crevices where hundreds of soldierfish hide. As you approach, these shy fish dart into the coral with such collective precision it is as if they were one. This single colony of coral, which stands more than 15 feet high, is also home to a family of clownfish living in a delicate anemone, which at times will close, exposing an underside as soft as a freshly ripe peach.

At the end of the channel a desert of sand stretches as far as the eye can see. Here colonies of garden eels gently wave in the current and at times a large stingray lies buried in the sand. You might even catch a glimpse of a shy leopard shark quietly swimming off into the distant lagoon.

Just east of the channel lies the historic island of Ulong — its high limestone cliffs, dense tropical jungle and perfect white sand beach just begging for a camera. In 1783 British captain Henry Wilson ran his merchant ship aground on the reef just north of this island. Wilson and his crew were able to salvage lifeboats and supplies and row to Ulong where they were greeted by a friendly chief, the Ibedul of Koror. The Ibedul offered assistance, the English offered tea and thus a lasting friendship began. Within three months the ship was repaired and Wilson returned to England with the chief's son, Lebuu, who became something of a celebrity until he died of smallpox several months later. A popular play was written about Lebuu and his grave can still be seen at St. Mary's Cathedral in Greenwich. Wilson's brief visit had a significant impact on Palau, but he left behind a questionable legacy. He not only introduced guns to the warring clans, which permanently changed the balance of power, but the reports of his experience opened the islands to further Western contact.

*L*ike *fish in deep, clear
water," goes one Belauan saying, "eaten only with the
eyes." This expression is often used when referring to things
that can only be admired from afar, like expensive items
in a store or another's spouse.*

Seasoned divers looking for an alternative to the crowded Blue
Corner are again diving Shark City for their thrills. Those in the know dive the
corner of the reef for an exciting drift through blue water and big schools of fish
— hundreds of jacks, barracuda, red snappers, black snappers, fusiliers everywhere,
monster tuna and huge bumphead parrots. This place is wild. You just never know
what to expect. But don't be misled by the name. Back in the late 1970s Shark
City was known for its schools of aggressive grey reef sharks that often prevented
divers from even getting in the water. Today you might see but one lone shark
swimming off in the distance. Large schools of sharks are rarely seen.

But the top of this reef starts in 60 feet of water, dropping to nearly 100 feet
at the corner. Add surface waters that can be rough and a current that at times can
be strong and you have a dive that's best left for experienced divers.

However, there is more to this reef than the corner. Some dive guides prefer
an area a little farther south of the corner where the reef grows to within 30 feet
of the surface and the current is rarely very strong. Here, beautiful fields of chalice
coral cover the top of the reef, you often see hawksbill turtles and, if you're lucky,
maybe you'll even see an eagle ray or two. Both of these areas are known as Shark
City so it gets a little confusing because they are as different as night and day.

Big schools of jacks, such as these bigeye trevally, Caranx sexfasciatus, *are a common sight
when diving the corner of the reef at Shark City. Photograph by Hiroshi Nagano*

*Long, long ago,
there was a goddess named Milad who taught
the people of Belau how to grow taro. Having done
so, she settled on the small island of Ngiptal just off
the shores of Babeldaob Island. Here, the gods
rewarded the old woman by giving her a magical
breadfruit tree with a hollow trunk and a broken limb.
With each new wave, fish were driven up through the
tree and landed in her front yard. In time, the people
became jealous and with clamshell axes cut down the
old woman's magic tree. As they chopped, the ocean
poured in through the severed trunk, flooding the
island which then sank below the sea. There, it is said,
the stone pathways and platforms of the village
lie in the clear lagoon to this day.*

In the distant past, after centuries of strong currents and violent
storm waves crashing against Palau's western barrier reef, a great underwater
cavern was formed. Gradually over the ages parts of its ceiling gave way, creating
four vertical chimneys — blue holes — that opened to the surface above. In time,
low-light reef organisms settled in the dark recesses of the cave and it became a
haven for rays, turtles, sleeping sharks and schools of fish. Today the Blue Hole is
legendary among underwater photographers for the dramatic light that fills the
cavern from above.

A short snorkel across the shallow reef top to any one of the four chimney

*Rays of sunlight filter down through vertical shafts of the Blue Hole and bathe this vast
underwater cavern in rich, warm light, providing a dramatic setting for available light
photography. Photograph by Hiroshi Nagano*

entrances is hardly preparation for the 80-foot free-fall through the body of the reef. As you slowly descend into this cathedral-like chamber, light diffuses through the spectrum from soft green to sapphire blue and disappears to indigo below. Here, solitary wire corals, some more than 20 feet long, hang from the ceiling of the cave while whitetip reef sharks occasionally lie on the sandy 110-foot bottom. A near-spiritual setting is created by the rays of sunlight that filter down through the vertical shafts. At times the water is so clear that a glance upward might even reveal the clouds overhead. In the rear of the cavern, a long, low tunnel leads to another chamber jokingly referred to as the Temple of Doom. This chamber is no joke. It's dark and dangerous and there is nothing inside. Also, its only opening is not visible once you swim down into the cave.

At 80 feet, a large, arched passage leads from the enormous central cavern out onto the face of a deep vertical dropoff. Below this exit a sandy area spills out from the floor of the cavern where bottom-dwelling leopard sharks, a harmless shark distinguised by the leopard-like spots covering its beige body, are sometimes seen.

Although you could easily spend your entire dive exploring the huge cavern and its surrounding reef, most guides like to combine this dive with a swim to Blue Corner, a popular dive site known for its sharks and big schools of fish. With this choice, however, you end up with only half of two good dives. The Blue Hole is quiet, completely different from the electrifying excitement of the famous Blue Corner. If you are a photographer or the kind of diver who likes to take your time, then perhaps you would enjoy spending the entire dive exploring the Blue Hole. Tell your guide to save the Blue Corner for another day.

There are a number of blue holes in Palau, but the most popular to dive is the group of four holes (pictured in the center of the aerial photograph) located along the southwestern barrier reef, just west of the Ngemelis Islands. The large peninsula of reef above the Blue Hole is Blue Corner, a dive site famous for its sharks and large schools of pelagic fish. Photograph by Ed Robinson

*T*here once lived a great
fisherman who went out to sea each day to fish for
sharks. One day, while he was far out at sea, a huge shark
began swimming next to his canoe with its belly toward the
surface. This unusual behavior was a sure sign that something
was not right. After much thought, the fisherman began to
suspect that his wife had been unfaithful. Angrily, he hurried
back to his village, devising a way to find the guilty man. As
he approached the dock where the men of the village gathered at
the end of each day, he raised his spear and shouted, "I know
which of you has been with my wife. Run, for your life is no
longer yours." The guilty man started to run, but foolishly he
had given himself away — the spear pierced his body before he
could flee. From that day on, no man in the village dared to
cross this clever fisherman again.

Since its discovery over a decade ago, Blue Corner has gained
a reputation as one of the finest dive sites in the world. With its huge schools
of fish and near constant parade of sharks, it's not hard to understand why.

Blue Corner is the tip of a large section of the western barrier reef that
juts far out into the blue open water of the Philippine Sea. When the incoming
current hits the steep vertical wall, nutrient-rich water is pushed toward the
surface and the food chain is set in motion. "The little fish comes out," explains

Grey reef sharks, Carcharhinus amblyrhynchos, *like the one pictured here, are a common sight
at Blue Corner. What is not common, however, is the large school of Moorish idols,* Zanclus
cornutus. *Moorish idols generally feed in groups of four or five — rarely are they seen in schools
this large. At certain times of the year, generally the winter months of January, February and
March, large schools of Moorish idols appear along the reef at Blue Corner as well as New
Dropoff, Peleliu Corner and Short Dropoff. Photograph by Hiroshi Nagano*

a veteran Palauan dive operator, "the big fish comes up, the bigger fish comes in, and the sharks are feeding on the rest."

More than 20 sharks are often seen just at the corner alone. Grey reefs are the most common species, however threshers and silvertips have also been reported. Even hammerheads have been seen in the very deep water. Nevertheless, thousands of divers have dived at Blue Corner without a single incident. These sharks see divers almost daily and seem to tolerate the constant intrusion. It's a wonder that *they* haven't been frightened away. But don't be misled by their seemingly nonchalant attitude. Many sharks, especially grey reefs, are very territorial.

But there is much more to this dive than the sharks. A hugh school of barracuda stalks the corner of the reef, often moving away from the dropoff when divers are in the water, forming its own shimmering silver wall. And an enormous school of jacks hangs in the deep water over 100 feet, their silver bodies forming a dense swirling mass. During the winter months between January and March, schools of colorful Moorish idols, graceful fish rarely seen in schools, appear along this reef — often accompanied by even larger schools of garishly clad divers. This is the most popular dive in Palau, so don't expect to be the only one on the reef. But even with all the divers, the fish just keep on coming. Iridescent blue fusiliers pour down the reef like flowing waterfalls while hundreds of pyramid butterflyfish flutter along the edge of the dropoff. Schools of snapper, rainbow runners and redtooth triggers swarm in the confusion along with big, beautiful humpnose unicornfish with long graceful tails. Monster tuna sweep in from the open ocean and occasionally you will see mantas in the blue water just off the wall. Those

---

The resident school of barracuda, Sphyraena genie, *forms a flowing sculpture of silvery fish. Barracuda are large, voracious predators with needlelike teeth that protrude from their lower jaw, giving them a menacing look. They feed on small fish in the open water and are masters at making themselves invisible to their prey. When seen head-on their narrow profile looks small and unalarming so they can approach their prey unnoticed and attack with a sudden lunge. Their fierce expression belies the fact that barracuda are not particularly aggressive. Although curious at times, more often they move away from the dropoff when divers are in the water, seeking the safety of the blue water just off the wall. Photograph by Avi Klapfer*

with keen eyes might even spot a marlin. You name it — if it's found in Palau, it's probably been seen along this reef.

Though the corner of the reef can be approached from either side depending on the current, a typical dive begins at the buoy just south of the corner where the edge of the dropoff is in 20 feet of water. "Keep the wall on your right," the dive guides explain, "and the sharks on your left" as you drift along a vertical wall that drops hundreds of feet. The current becomes noticeably stronger as you near the corner of the reef, the schools of fish noticeably larger, so large that most divers like to stop at the edge of the dropoff and watch the show — a humbling experience when the current is strong. At times, the current is so strong that the only way to see all the fish is to grab onto the reef, a definite taboo in most dive areas of the world. Although it's a thrill watching all the fish, you end up flapping like a flag on a pole, all the while hoping that your regulator doesn't fly from your mouth and not even caring that you may be breaking the coral. More often, the current is not so strong and you can maintain your position at the edge of the dropoff by simply doing as the fish do — face into the current and use your fins. Also, there are obvious areas at the lip of the dropoff where there is no coral. If you must hang on, take care of yourself first but try to grab these dead areas to avoid further damage to the reef. And if you are comfortable in currents and don't believe in grabbing onto the coral, don't. Some of the dive guides have even made "reef hooks"— metal hooks attached to a small bit of line so they can hook into the reef and float free of the coral by holding onto the end of the line. These hooks are now for sale in some of the dive shops around town.

Among the special attractions at Blue Corner are the big Napoleon wrasses,

---

Blue Corner is famous for its dizzying numbers of fish. Equally as exciting as the huge schools of fish are the big Napoleon wrasses, Cheilinus undulatus, *one of the largest of all reef fish. Although they can grow to seven feet and weigh over 400 pounds, the ones most commonly seen are generally three to four feet long. Despite their size, Napoleon wrasses are often very wary and difficult to approach unless they have been fed by divers, in which case they will fearlessly follow divers in hopes of a handout. Adults often develop a prominent bump on their foreheads, hence the common name, humphead wrasse. Photograph by Hiroshi Nagano*

enormous turquoise-colored fish, often with a prominent bump on their forehead. These fish are huge — some of the biggest you'll see in Palau — partly because divers began feeding them several years ago. These once-wild animals now pathetically follow divers around in hopes of a handout and show no fear of people, which makes them easy targets for anyone who illegally fishes this reef. Feeding fish in an area where sharks are present is asking for trouble. There have been instances where feeding the wrasses has excited other fish, which in turn has excited the sharks. Think about it. Please do not feed these fish or support dive operators who do.

Even though the fish at Blue Corner get most of the attention, the reef itself is exceptional. Giant sea fans and ancient bushes of black coral adorn the dropoff at 80 feet. Graceful sea whips gently spill from the wall. Clownfish frolic among the flowing tentacles of their host anemones. And, at the corner itself, a garden of lavender soft corals blankets the vertical wall.

The reef flat on top of the corner can be just as much fun as the dropoff. Here, lethargic whitetip reef sharks lie in the open sand areas between the coral along with fields of garden eels rhythmically swaying with the current. Often a spotted eagle ray will gracefully glide by, while giant trevally herd schools of small fish through the river of sand that winds its way across the top of the reef.

Because the currents can be extreme at times, Blue Corner is recommended for experienced divers. And though the diving here is the most exciting when the currents are strong, currents or no currents, no matter when you dive Blue Corner there is always something to see — there's just not a more spectacular dive in Palau.

Schools of small devil rays, such as these Mobula diabolus, *often pass by the reef at Blue Corner during the winter months of December and January. Also during this time, schools with as many as 40 individuals have also been seen at Short Dropoff and Siaes Corner. These rays are smaller than the ones commonly seen in German Channel. Photograph by Ed Robinson*

*In Belau, the small
barracuda, mersaod, holds itself steady against
the current as the tide comes rushing off the reef. Suddenly
it attacks a small fish and just as quickly returns to its
place of quiet observation. This watchful, patient, almost
crafty approach to life is much admired as can be seen from
this popular Belauan proverb. "The male child, though
small, is yet like the small barracuda that braces
against the flowing water."*

New Dropoff, as the name suggests, is the newest addition to the
growing list of Palau's magnificent walls. Located along a large, rounded corner
of the southwestern barrier reef, this is a wild, wonderful dropoff where you are
likely to encounter everything from nudibranchs to grey reef sharks.

When the current picks up along this area of the reef, this dive can be as
exciting as the famous Blue Corner. Fish are everywhere, from colorful reef tropicals
to schooling jacks, snappers, silver barracuda and, at certain times of the year,
dogtooth tuna bigger than you. Grey reef sharks are so common that you almost
start to ignore them. On occasion, even silvertip sharks cruise by this reef. And
though rare, a small school of juvenile oceanic whitetips has been seen in water
deeper than most sensible people dive. Most of the big schools of fish gather near
the two large cuts in the reef about midway through the dive. Not surprisingly,

As if dusted by the morning frost, this beautiful variety of black coral, Antipathes sp.,
*is covered with tentacles of silvery white. Only the skeleton of black coral is actually black.
The animal's flesh may be yellow, orange, brown or white. Black coral is highly prized by
the jewelry industry and has become a rare sight on many of the world's reefs. Fortunately,
it is still found on many of the reefs in Palau. Photograph by Avi Klapfer*

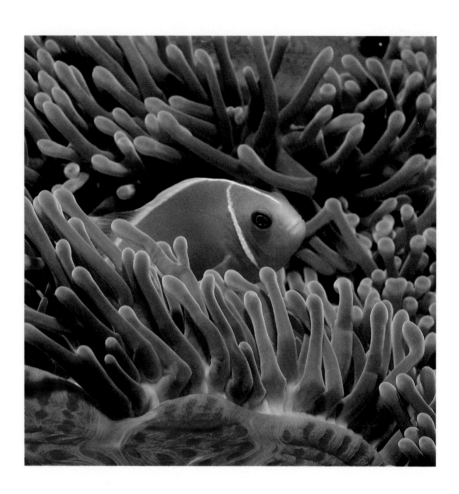

this is also where you'll encounter the strongest currents, including at times a slight down current in the second cut, so keep an eye on your depth gauge.

A buoy now marks the beginning of the dive where the reef starts in 20 feet of water. Here trees of elegant soft coral carpet the vertical wall while hundreds of yellowtail fusiliers linger just off the reef. Schools of pyramid butterflyfish and colorful anthias hover effortlessly in the current. A glance out to blue water might even reveal a spotted eagle ray quietly gliding by. At 80 feet, the sea fans grow healthy and large while deeper still, big stands of black coral grow between 100 and 130 feet, including a beautiful variety whose tentacles are white. Anemones, some as big as doormats, and their resident clownfish are everywhere. Some of the anemones have an underside of the softest shade of blue and, when they close, turn into luminescent balls of color.

As you near the end of the dive, guides usually head for the top of the reef. There is so much to see in just this area alone that you could easily spend an entire dive among the flame angels, fire gobies, butterflyfish and parrots, puffers, Moorish idols, yellow wrasses, even giant clams. Artfully camouflaged crabs, no bigger than your thumbnail, live hidden among the corals along with outrageously colored nudibranchs with gills of fluorescent orange and bodies a smooth velvety black. Herds of huge bumphead parrotfish forage among the corals along with schools of harlequin sweetlips and spotlight grunts. Whitetip reef sharks often cruise along the top of the reef where, if you're lucky, you might see the resident Napoleon wrasses, maybe even a turtle or two.

Surrounded by stinging tentacles powerful enough to kill tiny fish, the pink clownfish, Amphiprion perideraion, *is unaffected by the anemone's deadly toxin. Clownfish and anemones live together in an unusual symbiotic relationship. The tentacles of anemones are armed with microscopic harpoons called nematocysts that inject a paralyzing toxin into their prey. Clownfish are thought to be immune to these batteries of stinging capsules because of a protective mucus that covers their bodies, in effect making the fish chemically invisible to the anemone's deadly tentacles. Photograph by Hiroshi Nagano*

*Long ago, under the
soft light of a new moon, two lovers secretly met
on the island of Ngemelis. They talked far into the
night of their future together and finally fell asleep in
each other's arms. When they awoke the next morning,
the back piece of the girl's grass skirt was missing and there
were strange tracks near the spot where they had been sleeping.
Fearing they had been discovered, the girl quickly fixed her
skirt with the fronds of a coconut palm. The lovers then
parted, promising to meet again fifteen days later when
the moon would be full. On the appointed evening they met
again, and as they lay by the beach under the light of the full
moon, a turtle crawled up from the water and began making a
nest. To their surprise, fragments of the young girl's lost skirt
were entangled in its flipper. And thus it was discovered
that the egg-laying cycle of the turtle corresponds
to the phases of the moon.*

Back in the early 1970s when only marine biologists, anthropologists and a handful of divers had ever even heard of Palau, Douglas Faulkner was there photographing the wall at Ngemelis (Nem-e-lis). With the publication of *This Living Reef*, his classic book on Palau, the beauty of Ngemelis Dropoff was brought to the attention of the world. This spectacular reef, nicknamed Big Drop by the locals, drops straight down more than 800 feet, yet grows to within a whisper of the ocean's surface. Such a lush growth of marine life covers this wall that each dive offers something new and even more beautiful to see.

Ngemelis Dropoff is famous for its sheer vertical wall that drops more than 800 feet yet begins just several feet from the water's surface. Growing along this sheltered reef are some of the most beautiful sea fans in Palau. Photograph by Kevin Davidson

Ngemelis Dropoff begins just west of German Channel, the shallow pass that cuts through Palau's southwestern barrier reef. Its sheltered location offers a protected environment where sea fans and soft corals flourish. Its vertical face resembles an abstract painting as celebrated in a Faulkner photograph, where red encrusting sponges, pink tube corals and white lace ascidians form a brilliant mosaic of color and design.

One of the more beautiful times to dive the Big Drop is in the morning when the sun shines directly on this east-facing wall, illuminating the intense colors. Clownfish, anemones and brightly colored clams nestle among the golden fields of leather coral that cover the top of the reef. Wine red sea fans, purple soft corals and velvet green tree corals grow in as little as 10 feet of water, making the shallow areas a favorite with photographers as well as snorkelers. Sea fans of every variety adorn the vertical face of the wall, growing larger the deeper you descend.

The soft corals along this wall are some of the most beautiful in Palau. At times a gentle current flows along the reef, causing the soft corals to extend their polyps to feed. The reef becomes almost magical, for when feeding, many species of soft corals inflate their bodies with water, which increases their size dramatically. It's as if the reef blooms with field after field of these exquisite corals.

Grey reef sharks live in the deeper areas of the dropoff but it is not uncommon to see them in water as shallow as 10 feet cruising through small schools of jacks, snappers and electric blue fusiliers. But this is not the place to see hordes of pelagic fish. People dive the Big Drop because of its gorgeous sea fans, delicate soft corals and dazzling tropical fish — everywhere you look. Moorish idols, square-spot anthias, pyramid butterflys, colorful parrots, clown triggers, golden boxfish, spiny puffers and angels galore — this is the place to see all of those exotic tropicals that brought you to Palau in the first place.

Hidden among the delicate tentacles of a gorgonian sea fan, the longnose hawkfish, Oxycirrhites typus, *is rarely seen in water above 60 feet. Its tartan-like color pattern provides an effective camouflage among the black coral trees or large sea fans where the hawkfish makes its home. Photograph by Hiroshi Nagano*

*A*t one time in Belau,
men fished the lagoon with a huge net made from
the fronds of the coconut tree. Once the fish were cornered,
they were carefully driven into the osel, a small circular
trap within the net where they could be easily speared.
This difficult task required the efforts of many men,
and if mistakes were made insults would fly. Anyone of any
rank, chief included, would be targeted. Insults sometimes
involved another's mother — the ultimate offense. Although
swearing in this manner is not proper, insults among men
involved in any strenuous work are excused as
"tekoi el kereker," words of the lagoon.

German Channel is a long, shallow cut through the southwestern
barrier reef that leads from Palau's protected inner lagoon to the open ocean. The
channel was made nearly a century ago during the German administration of
Palau so that ships carrying phosphate mined from the southern islands of Angaur
and Peleliu could have a safe passage to Koror. Today it is still the only pass
through the southwestern barrier reef and is used almost daily by boats on their
way to the popular dive sites in southern Palau. Depth of the channel varies with
the tide but averages a mere 10 feet. As you approach the shallow reef, the deep
blue of the ocean water turns into rich shades of turquoise and aquamarine that
melt into the distant horizon of the cloud-filled sky.

Just outside the mouth of the channel the reef gently slopes to an 80-foot
sand bottom, forming a beautiful coral garden. Although the visibility here is

Manta rays, Manta birostris, *are plankton eaters and often gather to feed in German Channel*
on a changing tide. Photograph by Hiroshi Nagano

often murky and the scenery is not quite as dramatic without the sheer vertical walls, the beauty of this area is simply that there is so much to see. Enormous boulders of hard coral sit in stark contrast to the delicate fields of finger corals that cover the reef. Often a cuttlefish hovers above a branching staghorn or a lionfish hides beneath the overhang of a small plate coral. But what has made this area so popular is the recent discovery of manta cleaning stations — small outcroppings of coral near the mouth of the channel where mantas gather to be cleaned of parasites. Although you never can be sure a manta will appear, your best chance of seeing one will come from being patient. Once you reach the cleaning station, find a comfortable spot in the sand, make yourself invisible and wait. Often, from out of the distant gloom, the flowing movements of a manta's graceful wings will appear just within the limits of visibility. Soon the manta will circle, then hover above the coral while wrasses and butterflyfish clean parasites from its body. If you're lucky enough to see a manta here, remember to stay still. Swimming toward it or reaching out to touch it will only frighten the manta away. At times, grey reef sharks also come to this area to be cleaned, slowly circling the coral almost in a vertical position while small cleaning wrasses dart into and out of the shark's gaping mouth.

To be fair, not everyone likes this dive. Sometimes you see mantas. But sometimes you don't. What is often overlooked, however, is that this area is home to many animals that are not always seen along the dropoffs of the outer reef. The sweeping sand areas between the corals are alive with prawn gobies and symbiotic blind shrimp. Crocodilefish, strange-looking creatures with a snout like their namesake and big bulging eyes, lie in the coral rubble and debris, along with colonies of garden eels, shy animals that live in small tubes in the sand.

A striped barber-pole goby, Stonogobiops xanthorhinica, *stands guard near the entrance to its burrow while the colorful pistol shrimp,* Alpheus randalli, *goes about the never-ending chore of keeping their shared home free from debris. According to Dr. John McCosker of the California Academy of Sciences, this appears to represent the first Palauan record of these species. Photograph by Hiroshi Nagano*

*L*ong ago on the island
of Ngercheu, there lived a woman whose daughter
was about to give birth. Without warning, the old woman
died and her soul passed to the place where all spirits stop
to bathe before going on to the other side. She asked the others
at this place if she could go back to care for her daughter, for
in those days women in labor often died. The spirits agreed but
warned the old woman that once she left them she could never
return. So the old woman went back to care for her daughter,
who soon gave birth to a beautiful child. But food was scarce
on this barren rock island, and the new family nearly starved.
One day, a turtle crawled ashore and laid a nest of eggs.
Again and again the turtle returned, each time leaving a
fresh nest of eggs. And so the family was saved. To this
day, the spirit of the old woman still wanders the island
protecting her clan and their land. And the sacred turtle,
its shell now encrusted with a necklace of barnacles,
still lives, forever free from all harm.

Many of the islands in southern Palau are fringed by pristine
beaches that were once used as nesting grounds by hawksbill turtles. Such is the
case with the small, sheltered cove just west of the legendary island of Ngercheu.
Although turtles no longer lay their eggs along this beach, and it's rare that you'll
see one on the dive, their memory is kept alive through the name, Turtle Cove.

Several hundred yards off this secluded sand beach lies a vertical, coral-
covered reef that grows to within several feet of the water's surface. Here, an

Rivaling the beauty of any flower, the delicate tentacles of a tube coral, Tubastraea sp., *are usually
seen only at night. At times they expand during the day, however, in the relative darkness of the
overhanging ledges at Turtle Cove. Photograph by Al Giddings*

oval-shaped hole in the top of the reef marks the beginning of this beautiful dive. As you slowly drift down into the darkness of the hole, rays of sunlight reflect off the sandy bottom 70 feet below. A small window opens onto the reef at 25 feet, while deeper still, at the base of the tunnel, a larger opening spills out onto the vertical wall. Graceful schools of pyramid butterflyfish greet you as you swim from the tunnel out onto the dropoff, while Moorish idols feed among the orange tube corals and chrome yellow encrusting sponges.

Once out of the tunnel, you swim to the right along a deep vertical wall that reaches to within 30 feet of the surface. Golden sea fans, as delicate as lace, and feathery bushes of black coral adorn the face of a reef that is honeycombed with holes where nocturnal squirrelfish, soldierfish and bright orange bigeyes hover in the shadows. Red sea whips, purple soft corals and leather corals with fragile, daisy-like polyps add a riot of color and form. Here, a close look might reveal a grouper lying motionless on the reef, blending so well with its surroundings that it goes unnoticed until frightened away, or a tiny goby, barely half an inch long, scurrying among the fleshy polyps of a solitary wire coral. The resident school of black snapper — gunmetal grey with black fins, tails and eyes — moves along the reef as if in slow motion, while grey reef sharks cruise the blue open water just off the wall.

The reef makes a gradual turn to the right, where schools of fusiliers, black surgeonfish and colorful anthias gather in the current along with spectacular humpnose unicornfish with electric blue markings and long, graceful filaments flowing from their tails. Even a school of juvenile grey reef sharks, exact replicas of their parents yet only two feet in length, occasionally storms past this area. Your best chance of seeing a turtle will be near the end of the dive, as you head toward the shallow top of the reef. This is also one of the prettiest sections of the wall — the corals are healthy and varied, their colors even more vivid in the shallow depth.

The stately lionfish, Pterois volitans, *is among the most beautiful fish on the reef. Photograph by Murray Kaufman*

*L*ong ago, there lived
a wise old man who prepared a great feast for those
who had cared for him over the years. After the meal, he
surprised his guests with gifts of special coats that would
forever protect them from harm. One by one, he passed them
out — first to Ketat, the coconut crab, then to Rekung, the
land crab, then to Chemang, the mangrove crab. Chum, the
hermit crab, anxiously waited his turn for there was a special
coat that he wanted all his own. Suddenly, his heart stopped
for the old man unknowingly gave the prized garment to
someone else. With this, Chum grabbed the coat and put it on.
The others gasped in horror — so embarrassed were they by his
greedy behavior that they hit him until all the bones in his
lower back were smashed. Frightened and ashamed, Chum
escaped to the beach and crawled into the first shell he could
find. And to this day the hermit crab has no shell to call
his own. Instead, he must forever hide his broken body
in the discarded shells of others.

Ngedebus (Ned-e-boos) Dropoff is located south of Turtle Cove
along a healthy stretch of reef packed with corals and home to a thriving fish
population. The reef drops vertically in some areas, steeply slopes in others, and
throughout is dramatically cut with deep crevices. A buoy marks the beginning
of the dive where the dropoff starts in 20 feet of water. Here, the visibility is often
murky but soon clears as you drift along a colorful wall full of lace-like sea fans
and delicate soft corals. Near the beginning of the dive, the reef is thick with
giant sea fans and dense bushes of black coral that grow in the dim light at

Like a fountain of brilliant color softly flowing from the reef, the graceful arms of a red whip
coral gently spill from the wall. Photograph by Avi Klapfer

80 feet. Shy leopard sharks sometimes lie in the open sand areas between the corals along with lethargic whitetip reef sharks quietly passing away the hours. A little farther along the wall, there is a series of small caves between 110 and 130 feet where large groupers occasionally hide.

Brilliant red whip corals grow from the reef, their long, graceful arms gently spilling from the wall. Crinoids cling to the solitary wire corals that gently wave to the rhythm of the sea. Everywhere you look there are colorful fish, from the irresistible clown trigger and graceful Moorish idol, to the shy sling-jaw wrasse, whose paste-white face and black-painted eyes suggest a circus mime. In the shallow areas on top of the reef, large cuttlefish — intriguing creatures that resemble squid — are sometimes seen, while deeper on the dropoff, below 50 feet, look for the shy blue-girdled angel, a bright yellow fish with brilliant blue markings that is not often seen in Palau. If you're lucky, you might see one of the more comical sights along this dropoff — a batfish relentlessly pursuing a hawksbill turtle, anticipating and following its every move. According to local dive guides, the batfish's interest is apparently gastonomical as it appears to feed on the turtle's excrement.

About midway through the dive, a small point juts out into open ocean, creating just enough of a current to attract the larger schools of fish. Here, clouds of pyramid butterflys gather along the reef, their sheer numbers adding a whimsical touch to the dive. Grey reef sharks weave among schools of fusiliers and unicornfish, strange-looking creatures with a horn protruding from their forehead. Occasionally a school of barracuda hangs just off the point, and at times, a roving pack of juvenile grey reef sharks sweeps past the reef. Once you drift past this point the wall is not quite as colorful, so many divers opt to explore the shallow top of the reef before heading out to blue water at the end of the dive.

Leopard sharks, Stegostoma varium, *are bottom-dwelling sharks found only in the Indo-Pacific. They can grow to eight feet, but their tails make up almost half their length. Leopard sharks feed on molluscs and small crustaceans and are relatively harmless to divers. They are sluggish swimmers and prefer to lie motionless and unmolested on the sand bottom. Photograph by Bert and Jan Yates*

*I*n the most distant past,
there were demigods who traveled around the islands
of Belau, visiting one another and seeing to it that human
beings maintained their good behavior. During this time, there
was a demigod from the southern island of Peleliu who kept
a school of mullet fish as his pets. And from the big island
of Babeldaob in northern Belau, there was a demigod who
kept the strong current of the sea as his pet. On one visit the
two demigods decided to exchange pets. And so today in Belau,
during the season when the fish spawn, a large school of
mullet fish appears off the east coast of Babeldaob
while strong currents and big waves often pound
the southern shores of the Peleliu Island.

When diving the dropoff at Peleliu (Pe-le-lieu) Corner, you are on the southernmost tip of the barrier reef that surrounds Palau. On one side of you is the Philippine Sea, on the other, the great Pacific. This is wild, open ocean and the marine life is spectacular — big, beautiful sea fans, enormous stands of black coral, giant anemones, sharks, huge schools of fish, monster tuna, groupers, Napoleon wrasse and bumphead parrots so large that you can almost hear them as they bite into the coral.

But Peleliu Corner is equally as famous for its unpredictable surface currents that range from nonexistent to ripping. Also be aware that when the current is strong, you may encounter up-currents and down-drafts near certain points around the corner, so pay careful attention as your guide explains how to approach this dive. The diving here can be as challenging as it is exciting.

Schools of grey reef sharks, Carcharhinus amblyrhynchos, *are a common sight at the corner of the reef at Peleliu. Photograph by Kevin Davidson*

The corner of the reef, which only advanced divers should attempt, can be approached from either side, depending on the current. The more popular approach is from the western side — the actual section of the dropoff known as Peleliu Corner. Here the reef is rugged and exposed. You can almost feel the power of the sea. Solitary wire corals, twisted and bent, eerily extend over 10 feet from the vertical wall. Ancient stands of black coral in shades of silver, green and rust grow in the dim light between 80 and 130 feet. Though the wall itself is covered with life, it's the fish that steal the show. When the current is running, huge schools of jacks and snapper circle the corner as if in slow motion while grey reef sharks weave among schools of fusiliers, rainbow runners and strange-looking unicornfish. Enormous dogtooth tuna sweep in from the open ocean and, if you're lucky, Peleliu's elusive old grouper, over four feet long, will make an appearance. If that's not enough, the top of the reef is home to the palette surgeonfish, a dazzling neon-blue fish rarely seen at other dive sites in Palau.

The eastern side of the corner, actually the more beautiful side, is known as Peleliu Express, a subtle hint that the current can pull you away from the reef at the end of the dive. If the boats can't find you, you're on the "Peleliu Express" to the Philippines. Dive guides joke that if you don't bring an inflation tube then you better bring your passport because the next stop is Manila. This is no joke. Besides an inflation tube, you should also have a signaling device, such as a dive strobe or mirror, on the off chance you find yourself on an unexpected drift into the sunset. And always surface as a group — it will be easier for the boats to find you.

According to local fishermen, this corner of reef is one of the best-known spawning grounds for many of the fish found in Palau, especially several species of jacks and snappers of which, during certain times of the year, schools of fish numbering in the thousands can be seen. In his excellent book *Words of the Lagoon* Robert Johannes suggests why. On one side of the corner, there is a circular current that prevents the larvae from getting swept out to sea and, at the same time, holds them far enough away from the reef to avoid predation during their vulnerable larval stage. When the larvae become large and fast enough to significantly avoid predators, they can return to a suitable reef habitat. A tragic incident during World War II graphically illustrated the existence of this eddy. In 1944, American troops invaded Orange Beach on the southeastern side of the island, at that time heavily fortified by the Japanese. The ocean ran red with the blood of the fighting men. But instead of dispersing, the blood-red water moved all the way around the southern tip of the island, where a circling current confined it within a stationary pool that was visible for days. This same current confines the pelagic fish larvae to the spawning grounds.

But there is more to Peleliu than just diving the corner. Peleliu Wall, located south of the old military harbor, is a gorgeous section of reef — some say it's the most beautiful wall in Palau. Thousands of small yellow soft corals carpet the dropoff, giving the vertical wall an iridescent glow. Even though the currents in this area are rarely very strong, big schools of sweetlips, humpback snappers and fusiliers sweep past this reef along with dogtooth tuna and a grey reef shark or two. Snorkelers have even spotted marlin here.

Peleliu Coral Gardens is another favorite spot, located just offshore from the famous U.S. landing site on Orange Beach. Here, enormous boulders of coral grow from the gently sloping bottom where you're likely to find bullets and spent casings that have been lodged in the coral for more than 50 years.

One of the most intense battles of the Pacific war was waged on Peleliu in September of 1944. The fighting lasted more than two months, and some 11,000 Japanese and 1000 Americans lost their lives. Today the entire island is a natural museum and makes for a fascinating land tour between dives provided you notify your guide in advance. During the Japanese occupation here before the war, they turned the island's many natural caves into nearly impregnable fortresses by constructing walls of reinforced concrete to protect the entrances. Some of the larger caves were able to hold more than 1000 men and were even equipped with electric lighting, ventilating systems and radio communications. Today derelict tanks, machine guns and other heavy artillery are still scattered throughout the island — their rusting remains now being slowly reclaimed by the jungle. Most of the tour is by car, but if you're up to a rugged hike through the jungle, ask your guide to show you some of the more out-of-the-way caves where you are likely to find old canteens, bottles and other paraphernalia left from the war. It would be wise to stay with your guide when hiking to these remote caves though — it's easy to get lost and there still may be live ammunition scattered around the jungle.

A two-hour tour is hardly enough time to fully explore this historic island. Overnight accommodations, ranging from simple guest houses in town to island-style beach-front bungalows, are available, offering you the chance to explore Peleliu at a more leisurely pace — whether by hiking the jungle trails, touring the island by mountain bike or beachcombing along the miles of deserted, pristine shores. At the time of publication, there was even a new dive facility on the island. These are small, locally run businesses, so be sure to check with the Palau Visitors Authority for names, addresses and rates of the guest houses that are open for business.

The dazzling blue color of these palette surgeonfish, Paracanthurus hepatus, *is a striking sight along the reef. These fish are fairly uncommon in Micronesia according to Robert Myers, author of* Micronesian Reef Fishes, *and are often found in loose schools hovering near isolated branching coral heads. When frightened, they wedge themselves tightly within the finger-like branches. Photograph by Hiroshi Nagano*

*O*n the southwestern
shore of the island of Angaur, there is a place known
as Ngedloch Beach where the souls of the dead stop to bathe
before passing on to the other side. One day a man was
gathering pandanus leaves near this sacred place and came
upon a group of spirits holding a feast. The spirits, surprised
at being discovered, gave the man a beautifully carved wooden
bowl filled with taro as a gift for the people of his village.
But while the man was on his way home, the spirits took
away the taro and broke the wooden bowl so humans
would not see how well the souls lived and would
continue to prefer life to death.

The charming island of Angaur (Ang-our), the southernmost
island of the main Palau archipelago, offers divers a chance to explore reefs that
are rarely dived. In fact, this area is dived so infrequently that the dive sites are
just beginning to be identified by name — or *names* since each dive operator
seems to be christening the same reef with his own designation. The island is
surrounded by a fringing reef where turtles and big Napoleon wrasse are seen on
almost every dive. And because Angaur is located outside the barrier reef, large
pelagic sharks including tigers, hammerheads and oceanic whitetips occasionally
cruise by — but these encounters are rare.

One of Angaur's more popular dives is located along the island's north-
western corner, just off the statue of Santa Maria. Here, the water is often as rough
as the shoreline is rugged, but big schools of pelagic fish routinely pass by this
area including jacks, barracuda and giant dogtooth tuna that fishermen claim

Schools of colorful anthias add a playful touch to Angaur's reefs. Photograph by Hiroshi Nagano

weigh nearly 200 pounds. The reef generally begins within 30 to 40 feet of the surface and then steeply slopes off into the depths. This side of the island often gets pounded by heavy waves, and it shows. The top of the reef is almost barren, covered only with small, tightly packed coral heads. Big sea fans are almost nonexistent until 70 or 80 feet.

Lighthouse Wall, a steep dropoff located along the western shore, is a spectacular dive. Here schools of huge bumphead parrots and giant trevally leisurely swim along the wall together with schools of black snapper and Goldman's sweetlips. Small canyons and crevices cut deep into the reef providing a beautiful backdrop for colorful anthias and gorgeous flame angels, a small, striking red fish that is found all over Angaur's reefs.

One of Palau's most pristine coral gardens can be found along Angaur's southeastern shore. Every inch of this area is covered with healthy coral, and the fish are so unaccustomed to divers with scuba that giant barracuda and big trevally jacks come in from the open water to check out the strange noise. Also located along this shore is the wreck of the U.S. minesweeper *Perry* — one of the few American ships known to have sunk in Palau during the war — which reportedly lies in just over 100 feet of water. And Angaur's elders tell of an ancient wooden ship lying just off the southern reef. However, neither wreck has been found.

Though the diving is enjoyable, what really makes Angaur so special is the island itself. There is a certain magic to this place that you can almost feel as soon as your feet touch shore. The people are friendly, the pace is relaxing and the rugged, easygoing charm of the island's 200 residents is contagious. Along the southern shores, the peaceful waters of the pristine beaches contrast sharply with the thundering waves that crash against the rocky northern coastline where dramatic blowholes send water high into the air. If you're lucky, you might even catch a glimpse of the pack of wild monkeys — descendants of the ones brought nearly a century ago during the German administration when the island was heavily mined for phosphate. Today, the monkeys outnumber the residents two to one and are becoming something of a nuisance by raiding the community gardens of taro, papaya and bananas. The monkeys have even begun taking the locally grown betel nuts — way overstepping the limits of most Palauans' patience.

Because Angaur is located outside the barrier reef, nearly an hour and a half from Koror by boat, dive operators will make the trip only when the weather is calm. If you have the time, a more enjoyable way to see the island is to fly there and spend a day or two at one of the local guest houses where you will be treated like royalty. Meals of fried fish, rice, taro, fruits and Angaur's famous land crab with coconut milk will be prepared for you by the women of the village (be sure to request the special dinner). There is also a small local dive shop on the island where you can rent tanks and a boat with a guide, but you must notify them in advance. This is a small operation and is not set up for large groups. Also, you need to be a competent diver. There is not much emergency support on the island since radio communications with Koror are only available during certain hours of the day.

If you're not a diver but crave the excitement of watching schools of big fish, try snorkeling over one of Angaur's reefs. Green sea turtles, grey reef sharks and schools of barracuda often cruise along the edge of the dropoff. If you're lucky, you might even get a chance to swim with dolphins. The only way to see these big guys is to snorkel over the outer edge of the reef, so you'll have to rent a boat and a guide. But remember, the island is surrounded by open ocean, so pay attention to the currents. And never drift far from the boat.

After a morning of fun on an Angaur reef, park yourself in a hammock by the beach or rent a moped, an island-style bicycle, or a truck and local guide for a wonderful tour. Roads of crushed coral and lime circle the island, shaded by a tall canopy of coconut palms and ironwood trees that provide an almost boulevard-like feel. Peaceful beaches, thundering blowholes and panoramic views are among the attractions as are the old phosphate mines started by the Germans at the turn of the century. These abandoned quarries have now become large freshwater lakes home to birds and a few wandering saltwater crocodiles. Historical war relics are still scattered throughout the island, remnants of the battle that was fought here

during the war. Angaur was also the site of a U.S. air base, and today the remains of a nearly intact F-4 Corsair fighter and B-24 bombers lie in the dense jungle along the northern coast, protected by towering ironwood trees whose fascinating root structures are as interesting as the planes.

Diving and overnight accommodations can be arranged through Paradise Air, Palau's local airline, or through the tour operators in Koror. Angaur's generator runs only from 6:00 P.M. to midnight so bring a flashlight — and lots of mosquito repellent.

As the name implies, hawksbill turtles, Eretmochelys imbricata, *have a projecting, hawklike upper jaw. Turtles breathe air but can stay submerged for several hours as they sleep. When awake, they must surface every 10 to 30 minutes. If they are frightened or chased, however, they panic and must surface more often. If you're lucky enough to see a turtle in the wild, appreciate the special opportunity and don't harass it in any way. Historically, hawksbill turtles have played a significant role in Palauan culture. Their eggs have long been considered a delicacy, and their shells were molded into money plates called* toluk *and presented to women in certain traditional customs. Although hawksbills are listed as an endangered species world-wide, they are still common in Palau, but their numbers and average size have decreased in recent years. Photograph by Bert and Jan Yates*

*There once was a man
from the village of Ngerchemai who went out fishing.
Just as he arrived at his favorite spot and was about
to anchor his canoe, he noticed a large hawksbill, a turtle
prized for its shell from which special Belauan money is made.
Without a second thought, he dove into the water, knowing
full well that if he brought back a turtle of this size he would
be the big man of the village. After a great deal of effort, he
surfaced with the turtle, but when he turned to climb back
into his canoe, it was gone — instead it had drifted far
away. As he struggled toward the canoe with the turtle
in his arms, the canoe only drifted farther away. Finally
he let go of the turtle, but by then his canoe was so far
away that the humiliated fisherman had to swim
back to his village with neither turtle nor canoe.*

In Palau, just about any sloping reef covered with healthy corals
is called a coral garden. In fact, most of Palau is a coral garden. Though soft corals
and sea fans get much of the attention, scientists estimate that there are more than
400 species of stony coral alone — their intricate patterns, subtle colors and varied
shapes giving them a special beauty all their own.

Dive sites called Coral Gardens are found all over Palau, but the two
most popular are both located near the small island of Ngerchong, just east of
German Channel. The first, on the protected northern side, is often referred to as
Ngerchong Inside. Here, rolling fields of beautiful hard corals gently spill down
the sloping reef. Delicate finger corals and huge colonies of nubby club corals
provide shelter for juvenile batfish, sweetlips and small angels. The second Coral

The serenity of Palau's many coral gardens is reflected in this photograph by Ed Robinson.

Garden, often called Ngerchong Outside, is located on the eastern side of the island where large table corals, branching staghorns and boulders of brain coral cover the top of a shallow reef that steeply slopes off to great depths.

Coral reefs that are hundreds of feet high and millions of years old are the work of some of the smallest, yet simplest, members of the animal kingdom. An individual coral animal, or polyp, is nothing more than a fleshy sack topped by a sphincter-like mouth ringed with translucent tentacles. Each polyp extracts calcium and carbonate ions from the sea and deposits them around itself, creating a close-fitting cup of solid limestone. Given adequate food, sunlight and other environmental conditions, the polyp reproduces asexually by splitting into two polyps, then four, and so on until the individual has formed a colony, each colony contributing to the growth of the reef. Coral also reproduces by spawning — releasing eggs and sperm into the surrounding water. Fertilized eggs become planktonic larvae that eventually metamorphose and settle onto the reef as single coral polyps ready to begin a new coral colony.

Only the thin surface layer of the coral reef is alive. Underlying this living exterior are the skeletons of billions of plants and animals that have cemented together, forming the stone-like reef structure. Minute, single-celled algae called zooxanthellae live within the thin surface layer of the coral's delicate tissues. These require sunlight for photosynthesis and provide nutrients for the coral.

Many hard corals extend their fleshy tentacles only at night, which changes their appearance dramatically. During the day the polyps are withdrawn into their limestone skeletons, but a thin layer of the animal's flesh covers the entire coral colony at all times. Kicking or sitting or standing on a coral colony can tear and damage this delicate tissue which can then become infected with a harmful algae that can spread like a cancer. Although coral is amazingly resilient, severe or repeated injury can eventually lead to the death of an entire coral colony.

A graceful cuttlefish, Sepia *sp., hovers above the reef at Coral Gardens. Photograph by Hiroshi Nagano*

*R*alm taoch," *says one*
Belauan proverb, "Like estuary water that is brackish."
Estuary water consists of both saltwater and fresh
rain water and is therefore neither. Palauans apply
this saying to a person who is indecisive or one
who only partly accepts responsibility.

It doesn't get much stranger than this — millions of harmless jellyfish, the size of softballs, silently pulsing around you, bumping into your mask, slipping between your hands and softly brushing against your skin. These unusual jellyfish, with stings too weak for all but the most sensitive person to feel, live in Jellyfish Lake, a landlocked saltwater lake in Palau.

The jellyfish in the lake are members of the genus *Mastigias,* a jellyfish commonly found in the Palau Lagoon with long, club-like tentacles and a powerful sting. Millions of years ago, ancestors of these jellyfish became trapped in what is now Jellyfish Lake when a submerged reef rose from the sea, creating a landlocked saltwater lake. Over the centuries, the long tentacles of the jellyfish gradually evolved into stubby appendages and the jellyfish lost their ability to sting. For food, they came to rely solely on the symbiotic algae that live within their tissues to capture energy from the sun and transform it into nutrients. To ensure that the

Of the more than 70 saltwater lakes in Palau, Jellyfish Lake is the most popular. Here, a species of jellyfish trapped in the lake millions of years ago has lost its ability to sting. Each day, the school of jellyfish travels across the lake in search of sun to ensure that the symbiotic algae living within their tissues receive enough sunlight for photosynthesis to occur. Finding the school often takes some effort, but with a little perseverance, divers often encounter a "wall" of these delightful medusae. Hamner and Hauri, the scientists who have done the most extensive studies on the lake, estimate the school to number more than 1.6 million. Photograph by Hiroshi Nagano

algae receive enough sunlight for photosynthesis, the jellyfish swim near the surface of the water during the day. Every morning the school of jellyfish, estimated to number more than 1.6 million, migrates across the lake to the opposite shore, and as it does each jellyfish rotates so that the algae on all sides of its bell are exposed to the sun. In the afternoon the jellyfish turn and swim back across the lake and at night they descend to the lake's middle layer, possibly to absorb nitrogen to fertilize the algae that grow within their tissues. The lake is also home to another harmless species of jellyfish, the disk-shaped, transparent moon jellyfish, *Aurelia aurita,* as well as sponges, mussels, small fishes and predatory sea anemones that live near the shore devouring wayward jellyfish at every possible chance.

Jellyfish Lake is located in the interior of the island of Eil Malk, a large uninhabited rock island about 30 minutes from Koror by boat. Once you reach the island, just getting to the lake is an adventure in itself requiring a 15-minute hike over a steep jungled ridge that is littered with sharp limestone and slippery decaying leaves. There are also several tall poisonous trees near the beginning of the trail whose trunks ooze an obvious black, sticky sap that blisters skin so watch where you put your hands. The jellyfish swim near the surface during the day so all you need is snorkeling gear. If you feel like lugging your scuba equipment over the ridge, be aware that even though the upper half of the lake is a harmless mix of saltwater and fresh rain water, at 50 feet there is a bacterial layer of anoxic water laced with highly toxic concentrations of hydrogen sulfide that can make you sick. If you dive, stay shallow.

Once you reach the lake, the search for the elusive school of jellyfish begins with a short snorkel through a small, mangrove-lined channel whose depth and visibility is only three feet. The school of jellyfish moves throughout the day, and finding them often requires a swim of several hundred yards through a hazy mixture of saltwater and fresh rain water where visibility is only 15 feet. As you search the water for signs of life, an eerie silence permeates the air, broken only by the occasional sounds of birds overhead. Just as you begin to wonder what you are doing in this jungle-enclosed lake, and if the rumor about the saltwater crocodile is true, a jellyfish often pulses into view. Then another, and another. Soon you are surrounded by a cloud of golden medusae. As you swim among these fragile creatures, use as little movement as possible — even a gentle kick with your fins can send them somersaulting through the water, and their delicate tissues are easily torn. Sadly, some divers throw the jellyfish around like softballs or remove them from the lake and dump them in the outer lagoon, where they have no chance for survival. This distinct form of jellyfish is not known to exist anywhere else. Its private universe has remained untouched for thousands of years. It would be tragic to see its numbers reduced by human curiosity and ignorance.

*There once was a great
fight between the fish and the taro plant in which
the fish was victorious. The giant Tridacna clam, Kim,
the respected one, was not at the fight and would ask
any passerby, "Who won?" But each passerby would only
answer, "Ask the next one coming." Then came the stingray
who got so irritated at the clam's question that he angrily
responded, "Why do you lie there like an old woman —
always asking and never doing?" He then stung her and
left. With this, Kim sent word to the chief, informing him
where the mighty stingray feeds. And on the night of
the full moon, the chief and his men went to this secret
reef and speared all the feeding rays. Satisfied, the clam
told the men to go sell the stingray, but only for the
smallest amount of Belauan money. And to this day,
the once mighty stingray is a fish of little worth.*

Just off the shore of one of Palau's beautiful Rock Islands, Ngchelobel, more than a hundred giant clams live in 10 to 30 feet of water. Boats often stop here after a day on the outer barrier reef so that divers can snorkel among these colossal creatures, the largest bivalve molluscs in the world. Giant

At Clam City, a garden of giant clams thrives in 10 to 30 feet of water. Giant clams such as the one pictured here, Tridacna gigas, *can grow up to four-and-a-half feet long and weigh as much as 450 pounds. Clams have survived years of subsistence fishing, but until recently they were becoming a rare sight in many areas due to poaching by both foreign and local fishermen. However a highly successful research project at Palau's marine lab, The Micronesian Mariculture Demonstration Center, has pioneered methods of breeding these giants, thus relieving some of the commercial pressure on wild clam populations. If you want to do your part to help re-seed Palau's reefs, several of the local dive shops have established a program where you can purchase a clam from the farm and plant it at your favorite dive site. Photograph by Hiroshi Nagano*

clams such as these are becoming a rare sight in much of the Indo-Pacific because of massive commercial exploitation. Palau has escaped this devastation and is one of the few places in the world where many giant clams can still be seen. Although most of the clams at Clam City were transplanted here from other areas of the reef for the enjoyment of the family who oversees the island, they are now thriving in their new location under the family's watchful eye. Don't even think about clam sushi.

It is not uncommon for clams to be moved from one area of the reef to another. In the not-so-distant past, Palauans would transplant large clams to protected lagoon waters to be used as a source of fresh meat when stormy weather prevented fishing on the outer barrier reef. In addition to providing a valuable food source — most of the clam's flesh can be eaten either raw or cooked or in dried form — the large, heavy shells were used to make blades for the adze, the traditional tool of the men, and pestles for crushing taro and tapioca.

Giant clams can grow up to four-and-a-half feet long and weigh as much as 450 pounds. But not all clams are giants — there are eight species, seven of which live in Palau, from enormous *Tridacna gigas* to tiny *T. crocea*, whose shell barely reaches a length of six inches. Regardless of their size, all clams receive their nutrients from the symbiotic algae that grow within their tissues, so they must live in shallow, sunlit areas of the reef to keep the algae alive. Many of the smaller species are enclosed in coral so that only their mantles are exposed, while the larger clams lie on the open, sandy bottom of the reef.

Wild stories of giant killer clams notwithstanding, it is nearly impossible to get your hand or foot stuck inside their shells — the thick, fleshy mantle of the largest of these clams, *T. gigas,* prevents it from closing completely. Some of the smaller species, however, can quickly clamp shut on your fingers.

Giant clams, such as this Tridacna gigas, *can live for decades. Some of the larger clams may be more than a century old. Photograph by Bert and Jan Yates*

*I*n the most distant
past there was a spider demigod, Mengidabrutkoel,
who lived in a breadfruit tree. One day, he crawled
across his web into the wax apple tree, and once there,
he turned into a man. While eating the fruit of the tree,
he saw a beautiful young girl and fell so in love that
he came down from the tree and married her. Soon
afterwards she became pregnant. At that time, people
did not know how to deliver a baby except by slicing the
womb open with a bamboo knife. But when it came time
for the village women to slice the girl open, the spider
man refused to let them near his bride. While the
women stormed outside the house, and the men of the
village threw rocks and tried to kill the spider man, he
assisted in the first natural childbirth in Belau.

Chandelier Cave was once an air-filled cavern, possibly formed during the last Ice Age when the level of the sea was much lower. Today it is a fascinating underwater cave dripping with ancient stalactites. Palauans know the cave as *Iiel Temekai,* the Cave of the Grouper. Divers call it Chandelier Cave because of the glistening mineral deposits that hang from the ceiling in the first chamber.

Located just minutes from Koror by boat, the cave is a series of four chambers, each one cutting deeper into the island's interior than the last, with ceilings that rise above the water level. Its entrance lies just below the waterline where a small arched passage leads to a silent world where enormous stalactites pierce the surface of the water, some by as much as 15 feet. This can be a place of intense fascination or the scene of your worst nightmare, depending on how you feel

In the cave, enormous stalactites pierce the surface of the water. Photograph by Avi Klapfer

about diving inside a cave. Whatever your feelings, no one should explore this cave without a strong dive light and a knowledgeable guide.

A course layer of sand blankets the entrance to the cave, so use care not to stir up the silt. Although this sandy bottom slopes to a depth of 50 feet, there is little to see on the floor of the cavern, so most divers never drop much below 30 feet before beginning their ascent toward the first air-filled pocket in the ceiling of the cave. Dark, ominous shapes of ancient stalactites, their tips now partially submerged, begin to appear in the glow of your dive light as you swim through this hauntingly beautiful underwater maze.

Stalactites can only form in dry caves. As fresh rain water slowly seeps through the island above, it becomes acidic, dissolving the limestone rock and carrying it in solution until it reaches the ceiling of the cave below. There, the droplets of water collect and start to drip. As the water slowly evaporates, it leaves behind its load of calcium carbonate, eventually assuming the shape of a tapered column. Not all of the water evaporates, however. Some falls into the cavern below where it has created a lens of crystal-clear, fresh water that sits on top of the dense, saltwater base. Fresh air also filters through the porous limestone of the island above, providing safe, breathable air inside the cavern.

As you enter the final chamber, the floor of the cavern rises sharply so that at low tide you can stand with your head and shoulders out of the water. Although some dive guides will stop at this point, and many divers will have seen all that they came to see, if you are so inclined, you can remove your dive gear and walk — or crawl — through a passageway lined with slippery red mud leading to a completely dry chamber that winds hundreds of more feet through the island. Here, rivers of flowstone cascade from the wall like waterfalls frozen in time, while stalactites glisten like icicles from the ceiling above. Delicate, pencil-thin helectites grow in every direction and seem to defy gravity with their unusual twists and turns. This mystical, enchanting place is a world few people ever see.

In the rear of the cave, a completely dry chamber winds hundreds of feet through the island. Photograph by Avi Klapfer

There once was a young girl who was born during the wrong phase of the moon. The mother, fearing that her daughter's life would be full of misfortune, constantly reminded her of the proper conduct in life. But this was to no avail for the girl became pregnant one day. With this, the mother's nagging increased, for pregnant women have many taboos. One day, while her mother was away in the taro field, the girl picked a handful of nuts from a forbidden tree. When the mother suddenly appeared, the daughter, in her shame, hid the nuts in her mouth and ran into the sea. Her mother pleaded with her to come back, but when the girl finally surfaced, she had turned into a dugong. Then she disappeared. So today one can see in the jaws of the dugong a bulge that was once the nuts in the girl's mouth. When a dugong is caught, it breathes like a human. And when it is about to be killed, the tears of the crying daughter can be seen flowing from its eyes.

Lighthouse Channel is the main entrance to Malakal Harbor from the eastern side of Palau. Its Palauan name, *kesebekuu,* means moray eel, which is far more descriptive, for this natural channel gently winds through the reef like a graceful moray. The channel itself was once a popular dive but now people mostly dive here at night near Buoy No. 6 where a Japanese fishing boat sunk during the war lies covered with beautiful corals.

Unlike other starfish, which normally emerge from under rocks or ledges only at night, the blue starfish, Linckia laevigata, *is often seen in the shallow areas of the reef in the daylight hours. Photograph by Ed Robinson*

Lighthouse Channel has really taken a beating over the years. At one time, every inch of this channel was packed with beautiful corals, but back in the early 1970s much of the coral was devoured by the crown-of-thorns, a spine-covered starfish with as many as 16 arms. For nearly two years, thousands of them ate their way across many of the reefs in Palau, each starfish capable of destroying more than 60 square feet of reef per year. At first this was considered an ecological disaster, and steps were initiated to kill as many starfish as possible. A bounty of 20 cents an animal was offered and local divers began hauling as many starfish as they could find onto the deck of a metal barge where the animals fried to death in the hot sun — nearly 355,000 of them. Although today scientific opinion is split as to the cause of these outbreaks, everybody agrees that the crown-of-thorns problem is not new. What is new is the frequency with which the outbreaks are now occurring. Some scientists believe that these periodic devastations are natural and liken them to beneficial forest fires. The crown-of-thorns may help maintain the diversity of the reef by eating the hardier species of coral that would otherwise overgrow and kill the smaller, more delicate species. Another possible explanation put forth by biologist Dr. Chuck Birkeland of Guam argues that an overabundance of starfish is the result of unusual environmental conditions that favor a crown-of-thorns population explosion. After periods of heavy rains or development along shore, the increased nutrients from coastal runoff may nourish the phytoplankton upon which the starfish larvae feed. This greater abundance of food thereby allows more starfish than normal to survive.

Whether it was a natural phenomenon or a man-made disaster, it took nearly ten years for the corals to recover, and for several years Lighthouse Channel was

This spectacular anemone, its beauty acknowledged by its scientific name, Heteractis magnifica, *is among the largest of the anemones found in Palau. Individuals over three feet in diameter are often seen along the reef. This species of anemone often has a brightly colored underside and is capable of closing in on itself, forming a brilliant ball of color with only a tuft of tentacles exposed. The anemone's delicate appearance and graceful movements belie the fact that its tentacles possess a deadly toxin that can paralyze small fish. Its resident clownfish,* Amphiprion perideraion, *shown here, are immune to these stinging tentacles. Photograph by Kevin Davidson*

once more bursting with beautiful marine life. But today, it is again showing signs of stress. During the last few years, development in the nearby town of Koror has increased. And now more commercial boats anchor in Malakal Harbor — discharging oil and miscellaneous garbage that then flushes through the channel with the tide. Even so, a shallow drift through the channel still offers beautiful things to see — gorgeous nudibranchs, exotic lionfish, graceful anemones and their resident clownfish, and starfish in flaming reds and cobalt blues. Even the sea cucumbers are beautiful in Palau. The caramel-colored body of the leopard sea cucumber is covered with cinnamon spots surrounded by dark brown rings. When harassed, these normally lifeless creatures eject a mass of spaghetti-like threads that will stick to skin like glue. Young Palauan boys used to wrap their bare feet with layers of these thin, sticky threads which would soon mold to the shape of their feet, forming rubbery shoes that would protect them as they ran across the reef spearing fish. At the end of the day, their "shoes" could simply be rubbed off with sand.

The shallow sea grass area that surrounds Lighthouse Channel is one of the most important dugong habitats in Palau. At sunset these shy, elusive mammals often come in from deeper water to feed. But they are rarely seen. At one time, the dugong was hunted for its delicious meat, a delicacy allowed only to Palauans of the highest rank. A prized bracelet was made from the dugong vertebrae and could only be worn by the men from the high clan. Although rare, these bracelets can still be seen on the wrists of a few Palauan men today. This hierarchical restriction helped protect the dugongs from overhunting, but after World War II, this and many other traditional laws began to disappear. Today, dugongs are an endangered species. A recent aerial survey in Palau sighted only 26 animals. While this doesn't represent the entire population, scientists believe — and fishermen confirm — that the number of dugongs is declining. Although hunting is against the law, the illegal killing of dugongs for certain customs continues. If nothing is done to stop this, scientists predict the dugong will soon become extinct in Palau.

Brilliantly colored anthias are a striking sight along many of Palau's reefs. Photograph by Hiroshi Nagano

*L*ike *the chambered*
nautilus," goes one Belauan proverb, "injured by just
one touch." The chambered nautilus lives at great depths
in the open sea. But with one bump against a rock, its shell
breaks and the animal drifts to the surface and dies.
This proverb applies to a poor sport, one who doesn't
take a joke well or one who angers easily.

Short Dropoff is a short 20-minute boat ride from the main
town of Koror, hence the name. This enormous, U-shaped reef on the eastern side
of Palau has several places to dive — the most popular being the southwestern
corner where acres of sea fans, some of the largest you'll find in Palau, cascade
down the sloping wall as far as the eye can see.

Rarely do you find so many sea fans, so big, concentrated in one area. Less
dependent than other corals on light for growth, sea fans are often found in deep
water between 80 and 120 feet. Here at Short Dropoff, however, hundreds of sea
fans, many over 10 feet across, grow in as little as 30 feet of water. These fans thrive
along this current-swept reef, aligning their flat, mesh bodies at right angles to
the flowing water to maximize their ability to capture drifting planktonic prey.

Although the big fans are the main attraction, grey reef sharks are also a
common sight here, and when the current is strong, a huge school of barracuda
often gathers near the corner of the reef. During December and January, look for

One of the most beautiful of all shells, the chambered nautilus (Nautilus belauensis *pictured*
here) lives at depths as great as 2000 feet. Its spiral shell, which is lined with mother-of-pearl,
can be made up of as many as 38 chambers, but the animal itself lives only in the outermost
chamber. All of these chambers are connected by a thin tube which the animal uses to control its
buoyancy by regulating the ratio of gas to liquid in each chamber. Photograph by Avi Klapfer

schools of small devil rays, sometimes 20 to 40 strong. Large bumphead parrots, a fish often confused with the Napoleon wrasse because of the large bump on its forehead, feed along the top of a reef. And if you look closely between the corals, you might even find a crocodilefish, so reclusive by nature and generally so well camouflaged in the coral rubble that it is not often seen by divers. Even frogfish, unusual creatures who crawl across the coral on stubby front feet, have been found along this reef. At night, the scene changes completely, offering the chance to see slipper lobsters, oscellated lionfish and other creatures that often hide during the day.

Short Dropoff is located next to the Belau Trench, which at 27,000 feet is one of the deepest underwater trenches in the world. In the mid-1970s, the chambered nautilus, an animal related to the squid, octopus and cuttlefish, was discovered to be living deep along the wall at Short Dropoff. Since then, the area has been the site of extensive research on this beautiful, elusive animal. Of the seven known species of nautilus, at least two are believed to be found in Palau; *Nautilus pompilius* and *N. belauensis,* the largest of the species and thought to be endemic to Palau. The nautilus lives at depths between 200 and 2000 feet, so if you happen to see one in the wild, you're diving too deep. One of the first photographs of a living nautilus was taken in Palau in 1975 by Douglas Faulkner who trapped the animal in deep water, released it in shallow water, and photographed it as it slowly descended back into the depths.

Short Dropoff is also home to Palau's newest shipwreck, a Bertram fishing yacht with most of the film on board for an upcoming BBC television special on the nautilus. The ship, which sank in less than 10 minutes, was last seen slipping off a ledge at 300 feet, then continuing its fall down the steep vertical wall. The crew was rescued. The special had to be postponed.

Sea fans are very efficient feeders. When their tentacles are extended they almost touch, enabling them to catch most of the plankton that drifts through their branches. Their lightweight, airy design requires only a small amount of surface area for attachment to the reef, yet provides a large fan-shaped area for feeding. Their flexible skeleton allows them to bend in a current, enabling them to withstand areas of strong water movement. Photograph by Mitchell P. Warner

*L*ong, *long ago, there*
was a woman who had so angered her husband that
he set her adrift upon a bamboo raft. But the gods had warned
the woman of her husband's evil plot and instructed her to
gather a branch of the hibiscus tree and fill half a coconut
shell with ashes. This she did, and days later when the
woman had drifted far outside the reef, she scattered the ashes
over the ocean as the gods had advised. She then stuck the
hibiscus branch into the bottom of the sea and covered it with
the coconut shell. This created an island and the woman was
saved. The island is now known as Kayangel,
and the sacred hibiscus tree still grows.

Kayangel (Kai-an-gel), the northernmost group of islands in
Palau, is one of the most beautiful places on earth. Its four palm-covered islands,
each circled by white sand beaches, fringe a transparent, turquoise lagoon, forming
a picture-perfect coral atoll. Only one of the islands is inhabited. There are no
cars, no electricity and fewer than a hundred people.

Kayangel is two-and-a-half hours from Koror by boat. So few divers come
here that the dive sites are still unnamed. The reefs vary from gently sloping coral
gardens on the eastern side of the island to steep dropoffs near Ulach Pass, the main
channel on the western side. Green sea turtles, spotted eagle rays, hawksbills and
an occasional leopard shark are seen in the clear waters around this pass, as are a
number of giant clams. There is even a resident school of spinner dolphins just off
the mouth of the channel. On the eastern side, there are several deep blue holes,
one of which starts on top of the reef at 50 feet and opens onto the dropoff at well
over 200 feet. And along the northern reef, there is a vast stand of the beautiful

blue coral, *Heliopora coerulea,* that will bring coral enthusiasts to their knees.

Ngeruangel Reef, just north of Kayangel, is even more remote. Barely awash at high tide, the spits of sand that make up this small atoll are alive with one of the only two nesting colonies of the great crested tern in Palau. Underwater, giant fields of Acropora coral stretch as far as the eye can see, and several ships from the Second World War, badly blown apart from various salvage attempts, lie scattered about the shallow sand bottom.

Though the vertical dropoffs in southern Palau are far more dramatic, the diving in Kayangel has a different kind of appeal. Its coral reefs are nearly pristine, and the scenery above water is spectacular. Your footprints on one of these deserted, white sand beaches might be the first in a month. Even the sunsets here are somehow more beautiful.

Kayangel is perhaps all the more special because of the difficulty in getting there. Boat tours are expensive and the only airline service to the island is by seaplane — and only then when they can find someone who knows how to fly the plane. Dive operators occasionally offer a two-day trip with overnight camping on one of the uninhabited islands. A day trip to the area can also be arranged, but boats leave Koror around 7:00 A.M. and return around 5:00 P.M. It's a long ride that doesn't leave much time to experience the peacefulness of the islands. Also, Kayangel is located outside the barrier reef so the diving, not to mention the return trip to Koror, is completely at the mercy of the weather.

Not many people see this part of Palau, but the extra time and expense it takes to get there is worth the effort. See it before someone builds a hotel.

Following page. Kayangel is a classic coral atoll, the remains of an ancient volcano that sank into the ocean eons ago. The evolution of an atoll begins when a volcano erupts at the surface, forming an island. Over time corals begin to settle on the volcano's submerged slopes, creating a fringing reef that surrounds the island. Over millennia, the volcanic island begins to sink back into the ocean due to its own weight pressing on the sea floor, but the reef continues to grow toward the surface. With earth movements and fluctuations in sea level, the reef becomes exposed to the air and vegetation forms. Today the four islands of Kayangel sit atop the rim of a submerged volcano. Photograph by Avi Klapfer

*I*n March of 1944, nearly 40 Japanese ships were destroyed at Palau during the American air strike Operation Desecrate One. Palau was an important naval base for the Japanese, becoming even more so following their devastating losses one month earlier at Truk Lagoon. Allied forces viewed this Japanese stronghold in Palau as a serious threat to their planned assault along the northern coast of New Guinea from where they planned to launch their invasion of the Philippines and finally Japan itself. Consequently, in the early morning hours of March 30, 1944, American warplanes, launched from the aircraft carriers of Task Force 58, began their relentless attack on Palau. For the next two days, they bombed, rocketed, torpedoed and strafed the Japanese ships, planes, buildings and airfields.

Tipped off to the impending American attack by Japanese spotter planes, several ships of the Imperial fleet made a daring escape through the American submarines that had surrounded the Palau Lagoon. American planes then laid aerial mines in the narrow shipping channels leading to the harbors and anchorages in the central island area thus preventing further escape. The remaining ships were trapped in the lagoon, and after two days of intense bombardment, they were hopelessly ablaze and sinking.

More ships were destroyed in the following months during the aircraft carrier raids of Operation Snapshot, July 25–27, and during the pre-landing strikes of Operation Stalemate II, prior to the invasion of the southern islands of Peleliu and Angaur in September of 1944. By the time the fighting finally stopped, more than 60 bombed and burned-out ships littered the Palau Lagoon. Palau's usefulness as a strategic Japanese naval base had been destroyed.

Soon after the war, the Japanese government and several independent companies began to salvage the ships. By the time salvage operations ended in the 1960s, much of the valuable information needed to identify and locate many of the wrecks had been lost, forgotten or destroyed. For the next decade, the ships were, for the most part, ignored.

In 1988, *Desecrate One, The Shipwrecks of Palau,* by Klaus Lindemann, spurred renewed interest. To research his book, Lindemann and local diver Francis Toribiong spent several years trying to locate and identify the wrecks. Then in 1991, Dan Bailey, an avid wreck diver and World War II enthusiast, published *WW II Wrecks of Palau,* the result of more than 16 years of diving and researching the ship and aircraft wrecks of Palau. But even with all of the recent research several of the ships have yet to be identified. A few have yet to be found.

Not all the ships that were sunk in Palau are diveable today. Several are lying upside down and are dangerous to enter. Some have been so blown apart — either during the war or later by salvage attempts — that they are now only twisted hulks of metal scattered about the lagoon floor. But some of the ships have been transformed into magnificient living reefs adorned with forests of black coral, brightly colored encrusting sponges and schools of fish.

Most of the ships lie in the protected waters of the Palau Lagoon, just minutes from Koror by boat. Many can be seen without diving any deeper than 100 feet. All are protected under the Palau Lagoon Monument Act; it is illegal to remove anything from the ships. Only three of the popular wrecks are discussed on the following pages. For additional information, refer to the excellent books mentioned above.

Preceding page. An attack photo taken on March 30, 1944, shows Japanese ships on fire and sinking. The ship at the top of the photograph, just left of the center margin, is the Amatsu Maru. *The ship with smoke billowing from her engine room, bottom center of photograph, is the* Iro. *Photograph courtesy of the U.S. National Archives 80-G-45323*

On March 31, 1944, after surviving a full day of intense raids by American fighter planes, the 470-foot Japanese tanker *Iro* was hit by two 1000 pound bombs and slowly sank to the bottom of Palau's western lagoon. Today, half a century later, this vestige of war has become a living testament to the endurance of nature. Hard and soft corals have overgrown much of the ship. Curious batfish follow divers as they explore her now-vacant corridors. Tangled branches of black coral trees hang from the twisted and bent railings. This abundance of marine life together with the interesting features of the ship have made the *Iro* the most popular wreck dive in Palau.

The *Iro* lies upright in 120 feet of water with her main deck between 80 and 90 feet. The ship was at anchor when she sank, and the coral-encrusted anchor chain still hangs from the starboard bow. Large bushes of black coral now partially camouflage the huge gaping hole where a bomb blew away a piece of the bow. Huge 5.5-inch guns, with barrels over 25 feet long, still remain on both the bow and the stern, mounted atop the skeletal steel framework of the enormous circular gun platforms. The *Iro's* center kingpost, which rises to within 25 feet of the surface, is packed with beautiful marine life including clownfish, anemones and rooster-comb oysters whose zigzag shells are covered with bright

According to author Dan Bailey, the Iro *suffered a bomb hit near her stern on March 30, 1944, but it wasn't until the following day when she was hit by two 1000-pound bombs—one along the port side, forward of amidships, and one along the aft starboard quarter — that she sank. This photograph, believed to have been taken several hours later, shows the* Iro *sinking stern first. The huge gaping hole in her bow, clearly visible in this photograph, is now adorned with the tangled branches of black coral trees. Photograph courtesy of the U.S. National Archives 80-G-45 321*

red encrusting sponges. Three giant clams have even settled on top one of the vertical masts — precariously balanced 45 feet above the main deck.

The *Iro* was a valuable ship for the Japanese fleet, for unlike other tankers which only carried oil, the *Iro* had two large forward holds that carried supplies and munitions as well. Today, these cargo holds are open and easy to swim into, but both are blanketed with a thick layer of fine sediment that can quickly reduce visibility when kicked up. One of the holds contains Japanese beer bottles and old leather boots that have been buried deep in the muck for more than 50 years. The bridge area is open and inviting to the avid wreck diver, but most of the ship's instruments have been stripped. Long passageways and numerous rooms on the deck level of the superstructure offer other interesting areas to explore. The engine room was heavily damaged by the bomb hits and resulting fire (as seen in the photograph that opens this chapter) and by salvage operations after the war. The ship's enormous stack has fallen on its side and is now flattened against the main deck. However, the four tall air vents that supplied the engine room with fresh air still remain in place. At the rear of the ship, the large tripod mast that supported the hoses used to refuel ships at sea still stands and is now overgrown with encrusting sponges and corals.

The Iro, *built in 1922, was more than 20 years old by the time she sank, and badly in need of repair. She had been hit and repaired twice during the previous years and then was hit again by a torpedo only nine days earlier as she was steaming her way to Palau. (Oil tankers such as the* Iro *were prime targets for U.S. submarines.) She was practically inoperative by the time she limped into Palau's western lagoon and was awaiting repairs when planes from Task Force 58 appeared on the horizon. Today, the massive stern gun, its barrel over 25 feet long, is overgrown with marine life. Photograph by Dan Bailey*

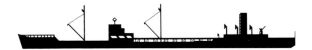

The *Amatsu Maru* is a huge ship, so huge that it takes more than one dive to fully explore her enormous 500-foot-long hull. This important tanker, so vital to the Japanese fleet, had been in service less than four months when U.S. planes attacked her on the morning of March 30, 1944. Two 1000-pound bombs tore into her hull, one in the center of the bow and one on the fantail. An intense fire erupted, engulfing the ship in heavy black smoke. A short time later, a third bomb made a direct hit in the middle of the ship and the *Amatsu Maru* began sinking to the bottom of the Palau Lagoon. Today she lies upright in 130 feet of water and is covered with such a dense forest of black coral that she is locally known as the Black Coral Wreck.

A heavy layer of sediment now blankets the hull, giving the ship a dark and foreboding feel. Wispy trees of black coral hang in the stillness, adding an eerie quality to the vacant corridors. Her main deck, lying between 90 and 100 feet, is littered with the empty shells of oysters and mussels that have fallen from the railings and upper reaches of the superstructure above. The forward face of the bridge, three decks high, has grown into a living wall of black coral trees, some

---

The Amatsu Maru *was built in 1943 as part of Japan's wartime emergency shipbuilding program. Ships carrying the suffix "Maru" were commercial vessels requisitioned by the Japanese military for use during the war. Military ships used a single name. The* Amatsu Maru *was specifically designed to outrun American submarines which had been taking a heavy toll on Japanese ships that supplied the important crude oil needed to sustain the war effort. She arrived in Palau only three days prior to the American air strike, loaded with nearly 7000 tons of oil. It is not clear how much, if any, of her oil had been off-loaded by the time she was hit on the morning of March 30, 1944. Today she lies on the 100 foot bottom of the Palau Lagoon. Photograph by Dan Bailey*

six to eight feet tall. Red snapper and skipjack school at the bow of the ship, and lionfish hover in the shadows of the rusting hull.

The superstructure, located just forward of amidships, is open and easy to swim into — the large glass windows of the pilot house are gone and most of the interior wooden decking has deteriorated, creating a large open space in which to explore. Inside, the remains of the ship's communications room can be seen, and commodes lie scattered among the loose wiring and debris. Unlike most of the other wrecks in Palau, little salvage work has been done on this ship. Although the masts have been cut, and the anchors, ship's telegraph and compass have been removed, most of the destruction was the result of bomb hits during the war. The stern area was heavily damaged and is now a confusing array of tumbled grated walkways and fallen metal support beams. The enormous propeller, however, remains intact. Lying in 110 to 120 feet of water, its four massive blades have a diameter of over 16 feet — an imposing sight in the cloud of fog-like sediment that hangs above the lagoon floor.

Although exploring the interior corridors and passageways of the Amatsu Maru *can be exciting, use caution when swimming through these areas. The heavy layer of fine sediment that blankets most of these spaces can easily be stirred up by a careless kick of a fin or even the most gentle of movements. Photograph by Dan Bailey*

One of the prettiest shipwrecks in Palau is the Japanese fishing boat that lies near Buoy Marker No. 6 in Lighthouse Channel. Although small, less than a hundred feet long, it is covered with a lush growth of coral. The ship was once fitted with a bow gun, which has since been removed, so it was probably used as a coastal patrol boat until it was sunk during the war.

Today she sits upright in 80 feet of water. The pilot house is overflowing with gorgeous sea fans and delicate soft corals. Green pipe corals, as smooth as velvet, grow from the rusting hull while schools of silvery bait fish fill the large forward hold. The main deck, between 60 and 70 feet deep, is swarming with colorful tropicals including angels, Moorish idols and the spectacular square-spot anthias, the female a golden orange and the male a shocking pink highlighted with a purple square that glows like neon.

This dive is even more beautiful at night when the ship blooms with basket stars, orange tube corals and the expanded polyps of feeding corals. But night or day, strong currents run through this channel, so the ship is best seen at slack tide.

According to author Dan Bailey, the Buoy No. 6 Wreck was once part of the Japanese South Seas Pearling Company fleet and was used to collect oysters that were commercially grown on the pearl farms near Koror. This photograph shows the heavy growth of hard and soft corals that now cover the ship. Photograph by Avi Klapfer

Survival in the marine environment
depends not only on an animal's ability to capture food but also on its ability to
defend itself. The feeding and defense mechanisms of many marine animals are
just as effective against humans as they are against their natural predators and
prey. Knowledge of an animal's behavior and respect for its environment are
the best ways to avoid potential harm. Many of the following animals are often
encountered with little risk.

HYDROIDS Hydroids can sting. Although these harmless-looking animals vary
in appearance, the hydroids in Palau you quickly learn to avoid resemble light
brown fern-like clusters. Hydroids, which are related to corals and jellyfish,
contain nematocysts, potent stinging capsules that cause a burning pain when
touched. This pain usually disappears quickly, but red welts or blisters often
appear on the skin, and an annoying rash usually develops.

FIRE CORAL Fire coral, as the name suggests, causes a painful burning sensation
when touched. Although it can take many shapes, from branching finger-like
projections to flat plate-like formations, its distinguishing features are its dull
mustard brown color, its white tips and the fine hair-like polyps that extend from
its surfaces. These polyps contain nematocysts that can inject irritating toxins into
the skin. The resulting burning sensation usually disappears in a few hours, but

---

*Top left. Although they look like nothing more than harmless plants, hydroids are actually
colonies of small animals that can give divers a nasty sting. Photograph by Avi Klapfer. Top
right. As the name suggests, the crown-of-thorns starfish,* Acanthaster planci, *is covered with
sharp thorns coated with a venomous mucus. Photograph by Kevin Davidson. Bottom. Hidden
within the delicate, feathery plumage of the lionfish* (Pterois antennata *pictured here) are long,
needle-sharp spines that can inject a highly toxic venom. Photograph by Murray Kaufman*

red welts may appear. Hydrocortisone cream helps to relieve the itching.

CROWN-OF-THORNS STARFISH The infamous reputation of the crown-of-thorns starfish, *Acanthaster planci,* comes more from its ability to destroy a coral reef than from its potential hazard to divers. An army of these voracious starfish can turn a coral garden into a graveyard of limestone skeletons within days. But the crown-of-thorns is also covered with stout spines coated with a potent, venomous mucus. Puncture wounds can cause severe infections and should be treated by a doctor.

CONE SHELLS Hidden within the beautiful cone shell is an animal whose venom can kill. This venom, which can paralyze the respiratory system, is delivered by a poisonous dart that is shot through a retractable tubular mouth called a proboscis. Even though the proboscis is located at the narrow end of the shell, it is able to reach around and sting a hand holding the shell's large, broad end. There are more than 400 species of cone shells and most are not deadly, but it is often difficult to identify individual species because a layer of brown tissue covers many of the shells. If you are stung by a cone shell, any cone shell, securely wrap the wound and immediately go to the emergency room at the hospital in Koror.

TRIGGERFISH Both the mustache and pink-faced triggerfish are generally very shy and will keep a good distance between themselves and divers. But when they nest, these giant triggerfish become some of the most aggressive fish on the reef. Though only a foot long, they have been known to charge and bite divers who unknowingly drift within 30 feet of their nests. If you see one of these fish blowing in the sand, assume it is guarding a nest and respect its territory.

Top left. Although curious, the banded sea snake, Laticauda colubrina, *is generally non-aggressive and rarely attempts to bite, even when provoked. But its venom is more toxic than that of a cobra, and bites can be fatal. Photograph by Ed Robinson. Top right. The giant triggerfish,* Pseudobalistes flavimarginatus, *pictured here, is generally quite shy. When it has a nest, however, it has been known to charge and bite divers. Photograph by Kevin Davidson. Bottom. Pictured here are a few of the potentially dangerous cone shells found in Palau. Clockwise from upper left.* Conus striatus, C. omaria, C. geographus *(responsible for the most human fatalities),* C. aulicus, C. tulipa, C. marmoreus *and* C. textile. *Photo by Sam Sargent*

LIONFISH You have to work hard to get stung by a lionfish. These beautiful fish generally hide in crevices or under ledges during the day and rarely attack unless provoked. But if they feel threatened, they lower their heads and charge with lightning speed, stabbing their opponent with venomous spines hidden within their feathery plumage. Although this venom is rarely lethal, it can cause excruciating pain. Soaking the area in hot water helps inactivate the venom. If the pain persists, consult a doctor.

STONEFISH People rarely get stung by stonefish in Palau. It's a good thing, because a puncture wound can cause agonizing, almost unbearable pain. Some injuries have even been fatal. Stonefish, as the name suggests, look like rocks or coral-covered stones. They prefer to lie motionless under rocks or partially buried in the sand so they almost disappear within the reef. Most injuries occur when a diver accidentally places a hand or foot on them — for hidden in their warty skin are up to fourteen spines that can inject a highly toxic venom. If you are stung by a stonefish, soak the affected area in hot water and seek medical attention at the hospital in Koror immediately.

SHARKS Almost all tropical species of sharks are found in Palau but, to date, no unprovoked attacks on divers are known to have occurred. Although all sharks should be regarded with caution, most reef sharks that frequent the popular dive sites are accustomed to divers and present little danger as long as there is no spearfishing in the area. The species most often seen in Palau are blacktips, whitetips and grey reef sharks. Blacktip reef sharks, *Carcharhinus melanopterus,* have a distinctive black tip on their fins. They grow as long as six feet and can be inquisitive, but they tend to be shy and easily frightened. Whitetip reef sharks,

Top. Grey reef sharks, Carcharhinus amblyrhynchos, *which can grow to seven feet in length, are the most aggressive of the sharks commonly found on Palauan reefs. They can be recognized by the distinctive black trailing edge of the tail fin. Photograph by Hiroshi Nagano. Bottom. Unlike other sharks, which must swim constantly to keep oxygen-supplying water over their gills, the whitetip reef shark,* Triaenodon obesus, *can pump water over its gills while it remains motionless on the bottom. Photograph by Kevin Davidson*

Triaenodon obesus, have an obvious white tip on their dorsal and tail fins. These nonaggressive sharks are often found resting on flat, sandy areas of the reef or in caves to which they regularly return. Grey reef sharks, *Carcharhinus amblyrhynchos,* are the most territorial of the sharks commonly found on Palauan reefs. When threatened they display a distinctive aggressive posture — arched back, nose up, tail down — a clear warning to get out of their way. Schools of grey reef sharks may readily enter into a feeding frenzy when bait or speared fish are in the water.

SEA SNAKES Of the more than 50 species of sea snakes in the world, only one is found in Palau, the banded sea snake, *Laticauda colubrina.* Its silver body is marked with jet-black bands, its face is highlighted by a pale yellow snout. Although curious, these snakes are generally not aggressive and rarely bite, even when they are provoked. Their venom is highly toxic, however, and bites can be fatal. All sea snakes breathe air but banded sea snakes, unlike others, can move as easily on land as in the water. On rare occasions, you may see one sunning itself in the Rock Islands. If you are bitten by a sea snake, seek medical attention at the hospital in Koror immediately.

CROCODILES You have to try really hard to see a crocodile in the wild in Palau — most of them now live at the crocodile farm in town. A few isolated populations still exist, however, mainly in the rivers and mangrove swamps of Babeldaob and Peleliu, and in several of Palau's marine lakes. Crocodiles are not found on the offshore reefs where most of the dive sites are located. On rare occasions, however, they do show up around the Rock Islands. If you are lucky enough to see a crocodile in the wild, chances are it will be small and swimming in the opposite direction. If you see a large crocodile — they can grow to twenty feet — be hopeful you'll live to tell about it.

A small saltwater crocodile, crocodylus porosus, *rests on a coral head near a Rock Island beach. Rarely are you lucky enough to see a crocodile in the wild. Moments after this photograph was taken, the terrified animal disappeared. Photograph copyright Ed Robinson-Hawaiian Watercolors 1995*

*C*onservation is not a new concept in Palau. For centuries traditional laws helped maintain a balanced environment so that there would be a continuous supply of food. Fishing certain reefs during spawning season was not allowed, and many marine animals were taken only for village chiefs or for certain traditional customs. These laws were obeyed out of fear of the severe penalties that were levied against offenders.

Over the years there has been a gradual breakdown of these traditions. Modern, Western-style laws now regulate the taking of many marine species, but lack of funds and other enforcement problems have resulted in increased poaching. And to compound things, many Palauans resent outsiders coming in and telling them what they should do.

Even so, many Palauans are doing their best to preserve the fragile marine ecosystem of their islands. But as Palau's popularity as a tourist destination increases, they have an ever more difficult task. It has been said that tourism often destroys the very thing that attracts it. As visitors to these islands, it is our responsibility to do what we can to help ensure that their pristine natural beauty persists.

Recently, a group of noted marine scientists and conservationists chose Palau as one of the seven wonders of the underwater world. It was hoped that by focusing attention on Palau's unusually rich and diverse marine life, people the world over would better appreciate and want to protect this underwater natural treasure. You can help by joining the Palau Conservation Society (P.O. Box 1811, Koror, Palau 96940; phone/fax 680-488-3993) and following the guidelines recommended by Palau's Marine Resources Division:

MAINTAIN YOUR BUOYANCY Try to prevent your body and equipment from knocking or brushing against any marine life, especially sea fans and corals, by staying neutrally buoyant.

DO NOT TOUCH, GRAB, STAND ON OR BREAK CORAL Please be careful whenever you are near coral. It is very fragile and can be damaged easily.

BE CAREFUL ABOUT YOUR FIN WASH Sand can injure or cover and smother coral and small sea creatures so please make sure your fins do not kick up sand or backwash over coral.

DO NOT TURN OVER ROCKS Many small creatures live under rocks and can't live anywhere else. By turning over or moving rocks you could be destroying somebody's home.

DO NOT COLLECT SEA SHELLS OR CORAL Besides being illegal in Palau, collecting sea shells and dead coral robs some reef dwellers of a protective home.

DO NOT KILL, DAMAGE OR CHASE MARINE LIFE This should be self-explanatory, yet you still see some divers sticking knives into giant clams, chasing and riding sea turtles, killing sea urchins and fanning sea anemones.

COLLECT ANY TRASH IN THE WATER AND ON THE ROCK ISLANDS Trash left on the beach usually blows into the water where it can kill marine life. Please keep the ocean clean by taking all your trash with you and picking up any debris you encounter in the water.

PLEASE DO NOT FEED THE FISH Even though it has become a common practice, feeding fish turns them into pests. Certain species of fish even become aggressive toward divers as a result of being fed.

MAKE SURE YOUR BOAT USES A MOORING BUOY TO SECURE THE BOAT Dropping anchor to secure a boat often results in damage to the reef. Mooring buoys, however, provide a secure, "permanent anchor" for boats to tie up to and help to preserve the popular dive sites.

k Tegeler

*P*alau is known the world over for its magnificent diving, but the island's natural beauty invites other activities as well. Kayaking and sailing are beginning to catch on, and many other sightseeing options are currently available, from snorkeling in the enchanting Rock Islands to hiking the jungled trails of Babeldaob, from exploring mysterious stone monoliths to float plane trips to the northern atoll of Kayangel. New tour companies seem to be opening all the time, and often close just as quickly. For the most up-to-date information write or stop by the Palau Visitors Authority, P.O. Box 256, Koror, Palau 96940; phone (680) 488-2793; fax (680) 488-1453. Meanwhile, here are a few suggestions.

ROCK ISLANDS You haven't been to Palau until you've been to the Rock Islands. Do what it takes to get on a boat for a tour through these spectacular natural wonders. Whether it's snorkeling among giant clams, walking along a pristine beach or just cruising through a quiet, turquoise lagoon, enjoy Palau's beautiful scenery above water as well as below. Tours vary from two hours to a full day and every one is worth it. Check with the various dive or tour operators to see which excursion best fits your needs.

AERIAL TOURS Palau is breathtaking when seen from the air. Paradise Air offers two daily round-trip flights from Koror to the southern islands of Peleliu and Angaur on their twin-engine, nine-passenger plane. The entire trip takes less than two hours, and, along the way, provides an unforgettable view of the Rock Islands and the Ngemelis area dive sites. If you have a full day, you can catch the morning flight and deplane at either Peleliu or Angaur and return to Koror on the afternoon flight. You can also charter a plane for specialized sightseeing trips over the picturesque Seventy Islands or the magical northern atoll of Kayangel. Paradise Air has also recently begun operating a five-passenger seaplane that can fly you to the Rock Islands for a swim or to Kayangel for a dive on one of its hard-to-reach reefs. The seaplane is also ideal for aerial photography since it can fly slow and low. For schedules and prices contact Paradise Air, P.O. Box 488, Koror, Palau 96940; phone (680) 488-2348.

KAYAKING Palau's spectacular diving has overshadowed the potential for other sports, but sea kayaking is quietly catching on and with good reason. Nothing can compare to the peaceful feeling of floating next to one of the beautiful Rock Islands with the sounds of birds in nearby trees and colorful corals and tropical fish just inches below your feet. A small kayak can maneuver into secret places inaccessible to the larger speedboats, where you might discover hidden coves, quiet grottoes, secluded marine lakes or sunken Japanese seaplanes from the Second World War. Several small tour operators now offer half- or full-day kayak tours of the Rock Islands as well as overnight camping expeditions to the pristine beaches of southern Palau. Either way, kayaking will give you the freedom to explore Palau at your own pace. For more information contact Adventure Kayaking of Palau, P.O. Box 225, Koror, Palau 96940; phone (680) 488-1694; fax (680) 488-1725.

SAILING CHARTERS Palau Sail Charters offers day sails, sunset cruises and weeklong charters aboard their customized Cal 48 sloop, *Eclipse.* With sleeping accommodations for two couples or a family of three to five, they can show you a side of Palau that, until now, has been unavailable to tourists — from an overnight stay in the peaceful Rock Islands, to diving and snorkeling reefs where few others go, to an exhilarating sail to the northern island of Babeldaob. The boat is ideally appointed for families or divers traveling with noncertified friends, and comes equipped with compressor, tanks and kayaks on board. For rates and information on the wide choice of tour options available, contact Palau Sail Charter, P.O. Box 1716, Koror, Palau 96940; phone (680) 488-1505; fax (680) 488-1115.

HIKING The rugged trails of Babeldaob and the intriguing terrain of the Rock Islands offer some exciting hikes where you can explore Japanese caves from the Second World War, an abandoned lighthouse perched high above the hills or pieces of the legendary stone money of Yap in a sparkling limestone quarry. For the truly adventurous, sign up for a hike to Ngerdok Lake, home to one of Palau's largest populations of wild saltwater crocodiles, or hike to the sheer cliffs of Ulong Island to discover ancient cave paintings and breathtaking views of the western barrier reef. Contact Sam's Dive Tours, P.O. Box 428, Koror, Palau 96940; phone (680) 488-1062; fax (680) 488-5003.

MOUNTAIN BIKING The unpaved roads and lonely side trails of Babeldaob are perfect for serious mountain bikers, but to date there are no mountain bikes available for rent in Palau. But things are changing quickly. If you're interested in this kind of activity, you might have to bring your own bike, and it will take some effort to find a local guide, but first contact the Palau Visitors Authority to find out if any biking tours are currently available.

TOURING THE ISLAND OF BABELDAOB For those with a sense of adventure and an urge to see the "real" Palau, rent a car — preferably one with four-wheel drive — and explore the big island of Babeldaob. At the time of this writing, there were no maps, few signs, and the new, as yet unpaved road was not finished. But this undeveloped island offers unparalleled natural beauty — lush landscape, peaceful villages, and breathtaking views of the barrier reef — as well as rusting Japanese war relics from days gone by. Consider a drive to the quiet village of Ngeremlengui where you can hike to the local waterfall or check out the ancient stone platforms and walkways from an abandoned village. Or drive all the way to Melekeok for a walk along a pristine beach or a visit to its traditional *bai*. You can also stop by the village of Ngchesar where the last remaining war canoe in Palau guards the entrance to the dock. During periods of heavy rain, parts of the road wash out, so

The fragrant white blossoms of the plumeria tree are among the many beautiful tropical flowers that grow in Palau.

check with the rental car company to find out whether or not the roads are pass-able. With few road signs to point the way, you might feel more comfortable leaving the driving to someone else. If so, contact one of the many tour companies that offer tours of Babeldaob. Make sure, however, that you will be in a car or small van, as a bus is too big and impersonal for an intimate tour of this beautiful island.

NGARDMAU WATERFALL For a completely different experience from the sun and the sand of the Rock Islands, a hike through the rain forest of Babeldaob brings you to the largest waterfall in Palau, the Ngardmau Falls. At the time of publication, the best way to get there was by boat from Koror. The one-and-a-half hour ride will take you north along the western coast of Babeldaob where you'll see the remnants of prehistoric terraces carved deep into the rolling hillsides. If you plan your trip to coincide with high tide, the boat can motor past the main Ngardmau dock and wind its way through an intriguing mangrove channel, its banks lined with the tangled, exposed roots of the trees. Once you reach the village at the end of the channel, there are two ways to get to the falls. The upper trail is shorter but steeper. The lower trail is longer but more fun. The two-hour hike takes you through a tropical rain forest where miniature wild orchids, lush ferns and fascinating mushrooms grow along the jungled path and hundreds of forest birds thrive in the canopy of trees high overhead. On the way to the falls, you will cross ten wooden footbridges in various states of decay, each one an adventure in itself. At one point in the trail, you'll have to wade through a river that is knee-deep so dress accordingly. Once you reach the waterfall, which varies in strength depending on the amount of rain, there is a cool, refreshing pool. Those with a sense of adventure can even climb up the side of the falls for a better view. But be fore-warned — the rocks are slippery, it's a steep drop and you'll be hard-pressed to find someone to carry you out if you fall. If you plan on booking a tour to the Ngardmau Waterfall, be sure to make arrangements several days in advance.

A hike through the rain forest of Babeldaob brings you to the largest waterfall in Palau, the beautiful Ngardmau Waterfall.

STONE MONOLITHS OF BADRULCHAU One of the most impressive archaeological sites in Palau is located in the state of Ngerchelong at the northernmost tip of the big island of Babeldaob. Here, in the historic area known as Badrulchau (Bad-roolough), columns of massive stone pillars stand in the middle of a vast open plain overlooking the magnificent eastern barrier reef. Until the new road is completed, the only way to get to Badrulchau is by tour boat from Koror.

The monoliths vary in height from three to ten feet. Some are standing while others have fallen on their sides. The stones appear to be arranged in two groups of parallel lines, one clearly longer than the other. If connected, the two groups would meet at right angles, forming a distinct "L." Many of the monoliths in the longer column have grooves cut into their tops. All of these grooves run in the same north-south direction which led archaeologist Douglas Osborne to conclude that these stones were meant to be the foundations of a huge *bai.* Osborne suggests that the grooves could have been used to support large stringers for attaching a roof to the structure. He believes that at one time the tops of these monoliths were aligned horizontally, but over the intervening centuries, grade level changes have left them as they appear today. Another interesting aspect of these ancient stone pillars is that many of their bases lie buried deep into the ground, some by as much as four feet.

Standing at the foot of the "L" are six additional stones that are carved with distinct faces — large, sunken eyes and gaping mouths with fanged teeth. Although some of the faces seem menacing, a few appear to be almost smiling. All of these stones are placed so that they face one another, looking inward toward the center of a large imaginary courtyard.

Top left. Unusual-looking mushrooms, such as the ones pictured here, grow alongside the jungled trail that leads to the Ngardmau Waterfall. Top right. The insect-eating pitcher plant lures its victims inside its trap with sweet-smelling honey glands. After venturing inside, the unfortunate bug slips down into the water at the base of the pitcher and soon drowns, its decaying body providing food for the carnivorous plant. Bottom right. This "intriguing" mushroom is capped with a delicate lace-like veil. Bottom left. Another of the colorful mushrooms found in Palau.

If, in fact, these stones were the foundation of an enormous *bai*, why the *bai* was never completed remains a mystery to this day. Local legend, however, offers an explanation. Long ago the gods decided that *bai* should be built all over the islands of Palau. The gods of Ngerchelong, known as Uchelkedesadel and Iechadrengel, persuaded the other gods that the first *bai* should be built in their village. So one night the gods gathered at the bottom of the sea and built the *bai*. They then began moving it stone by stone to its final location, agreeing that they must finish before the dawn since gods could only work under the cover of darkness. One god was instructed to carve a sun for the new *bai*. But when another god saw how grand the *bai* was going to be, he became jealous and used his magic to create a rooster. The rooster then crowed, and on the seventh crow, the sun rose. Thus the gods could no longer work and were turned to stone. To this day, you can still see their faces and only the foundation columns of the unfinished *bai* are standing, the remaining pieces still lying at the bottom of the sea.

THE AIRAI BAI The oldest existing traditional *bai* in Palau is located in the village of Airai, about a twenty-minute drive from the town of Koror. Whether you rent a car, sign up for a tour or hire a taxi, it is well worth the trip, for this is one of the most spectacular examples of an authentic *bai* in Palau. It is believed that the Airai bai was built nearly 180 years ago, "as the elders recall." And though many of its parts have been repaired or replaced over the years, some of the original

---

Top left. Long ago, the people of Yap came to Palau to carve their stone money, the largest money in the world. This piece, however, which has a diameter of nearly ten feet, never made it to Yap and remains hidden in the jungles of Babeldaob. Photograph by Mitchell P. Warner Top right. Stone monoliths are located in villages throughout the island of Babeldaob as well as a few villages near Koror, but Palau's most impressive archaeological site is at Badrulchau where the stone face pictured here can be seen. Bottom right. In the northern village of Melekeok, a group of ancient stone carvings known as the Great Faces are located in the center of town at a site known as Odalmelech. It is believed that at one time there were nine of these stones, but during the Japanese administration several were moved. The largest of the stones stands more than eight feet tall, its menacing face eternally looking out to sea. Bottom left. Another of Palau's stone faces, known as the Mother and Child, is located in the village of Ngermid.

pieces still remain. It is a great credit to this community that they have kept the Airai bai in such remarkable shape.

The *bai,* a high peaked wood and thatch building, served as a meeting place for the governing elders of the community and was the central focus of each village. The large A-frame structure was built from heavy planks of wood that fit together in a complex system of joins that required no nails, screws or pegs. Each *bai* was constructed on top of a rectangular stone platform foundation, the floor of the building elevated several feet above this platform. The front gables and inside beams were carved and painted with figures depicting important stories from the village. Repetitive images, highly stylized and symbolic, decorated the outside. Only four colors were used to paint the building: red and ochre made from clay, black made from soot, and white made from lime. The carved and painted interior posts that line the sides of the *bai* were each capped with a flat, upturned piece of wood that was used as a shelf to store woven sleeping mats. The two fire pits in the center of the room helped keep the insects at bay and kept the men warm on damp, humid nights. Located in front of the *bai* was a square stone platform with stone backrests in each of the four corners. If the four top chiefs of the village were unable to resolve an important decision, they would continue negotiations while sitting at this platform until a consensus could be reached.

In accordance with tradition, village *bai* were not always made by village members. It was far more prestigious for a village to contract with another village to build its meeting hall. The price paid would therefore be made public which was an indirect way for the purchasing village to display its wealth to others. The villagers who contracted to do the work would gather the materials and build the

---

The oldest existing traditional bai *in Palau is located in the village of Airai, about a twenty-minute drive from the town of Koror. To get there, take the main road toward the airport, continue past the airport turnoff and follow the signs. The paved road soon turns into a dirt and gravel road that winds through the tranquil village of Airai. A sign marks the beginning of an ancient stone path that leads to the* bai. *There is an admission charge for viewing the* bai, *with additional fees charged for still or video photography.*

bai, except for the plank flooring and thatched roof, at their village. Once it was completed, they would disassemble the *bai* and transfer it to its permanent home where it would be reconstructed.

Modern *bai* still exist in villages throughout Palau, but the building materials now consist of wood and concrete. These *bai* serve the same function as the traditional *bai* though today the high chiefs are often joined by elected officials. In an effort to honor the importance of the Palauan cultural heritage, two *bai* were recently built in the traditional style. One stands on the museum grounds and was completed in March of 1991. The other, built in 1992, is located in the state of Melekeok. Currently construction is underway on a traditional *bai* being built in the village of Aimeliik and there are plans for traditional *bai* to be built in other villages as well.

SIGHTSEEING IN KOROR If you only have a few hours to spare, rent a car or hire a taxi and see the sights of Koror, the bustling capital of Palau. Start your tour at the Palau Visitors Authority where you can pick up some brochures, a map of Koror and plan your own itinerary. Most places of interest — the museum, jail and Senior Citizens Center — are within walking distance of each other, but if you want to visit the clam farm (the Micronesian Mariculture Demonstration Center) you'll need a car.

BELAU NATIONAL MUSEUM The exhibits at the Belau National Museum offer the finest collection of Palauan artifacts in this part of the world. Although many of

---

Top left. The carved and painted posts that line the interior sides of the bai *are capped with arm-like projections that were once used to store woven sleeping mats. The underside of each projection is decorated with a symbol of a huge spider, recalling the famous spider god who taught natural childbirth to the people of Palau. Top right. Men at the Senior Citizens Center work on an outrigger canoe. Bottom right. Highly stylized and symbolic images decorate the* bai. *The smiling face with money earrings is a representation of a demigod, Chedechuul, the god of construction. The circle with a cross inside symbolizes money and refers to the importance of wealth in Palauan society. The bottom image is a stylized rendering of a giant clamshell. Bottom left. Master canoe builder Ilapsis Edeluchel Eungel slowly carves out the inside of a outrigger canoe using an adze, the traditional tool of the men.*

the oldest and best examples of well-crafted Palauan artifacts were taken from the country at the turn of the century and are now displayed in German and British museums, the exhibits at the Belau Museum will enhance your appreciation of the Palauan culture. Upon entering the museum through its elaborately carved front door, you'll find examples of traditional Palauan money, shell tools, wooden serving bowls inlaid with mother-of-pearl and paintings from some of the country's well-known artists. There is also a traditional *bai*, or men's meeting hall, on the museum grounds. Built in 1991 using local materials gathered from around the islands, this *bai* is a beautiful example of old Palauan craftsmanship. The museum gift shop sells a wide assortment of books on Micronesia along with storyboards, wooden carvings, models of outrigger canoes and items woven from pandanus leaves. The museum is open from 8:00 to 11:00 A.M. and 1:00 to 4:00 P.M. on weekdays, 10:00 A.M. to 2:00 P.M. on Saturdays, and is closed Sundays and holidays. There is a nominal admission fee.

THE MMDC The Micronesian Maricultural Demonstration Center (MMDC) has won international acclaim for its work on the conservation of giant *Tridacna* clams. Established in 1973 to study commercially important and endangered marine species, the center grew into one of the world's leading research facilities on the cultivation of giant clams. Over the last decade, resident scientists pioneered methods of breeding clams in captivity, thus helping to stem the rapid depletion of this once-threatened species. The center now raises and sells young seed clams throughout the Pacific to help re-establish clam populations that have become nearly extinct in most other countries. The center has also taught sea farming technology to communities throughout Micronesia in the hopes of establishing a viable clam farm industry for food production and economic development. Other projects at the MMDC include research on farming edible fish and studies

---

Storyboards, which originated from the legends carved on the gables and crossbeams of the traditional bai, *have become the most popular art form in Palau today. These unique works of art are carved primarily by the inmates of the Koror jail. They are for sale at the jail, the museum and the Senior Citizens Center as well as the Duty Free Shop at the Palau Pacific Resort.*

on endangered sea turtles. The center maintains a twelve-acre sea farming complex where long cement raceways full of *Tridacnid* clams in various stages of development are on display as well as three species of endangered sea turtles, the hawksbill, green and loggerhead. The facility is open weekdays and charges a modest admission fee.

THE JAIL One of Koror's most colorful attractions is the local jail where inmates sell storyboards, carved pieces of wood that depict early Palauan legends. The jail has long been the source of well crafted storyboards, a tradition that began back in the early 1960s when one of the inmates, Baris Sylvester, a self-taught carver who spent most of his life in the Koror jail, refined the art of carving storyboards to the level of sophistication that appears today. During his incarceration, he taught many of his fellow inmates how to carve these unique works of art so that today most of the storyboards for sale in Koror were carved by current or former prison inmates. The jail is open from 8:00 A.M. until 4:00 P.M. daily but these hours could change so check with the Palau Visitors Authority before you go.

SENIOR CITIZENS CENTER For a glimpse of authentic Palauan community life, stop by the Senior Citizens Center where women gather in the open-air summerhouse and weave handbags, hats and betel nut bags. Just in front of the summerhouse there is a fine example of a traditional Palauan canoe house, or *diangel,* an open-sided thatch-roofed structure that is lashed together in the traditional style. Sitting inside is a recently finished outrigger canoe, one of the few remaining' traditional canoes in the islands. When visiting the center, keep in mind that this is not a tourist attraction. It is a place where seniors gather during the day to socialize. It's quiet. Visitors are welcome but don't expect to be shown around the facilities. If you are lucky, you might even find the women practicing for an upcoming dance performance or the men working on yet another outrigger canoe. The Omruul Gift Shop, adjacent to the center, has an excellent selection of authentic

Fascinating trees, like the one pictured here from the island of Angaur, grow throughout the jungles of Palau.

Palauan crafts woven from palm and pandanus leaves. There is also a good selection of storyboards and additional items made by the senior citizens. Tortoiseshell jewelry is also for sale here, but it is illegal to take tortoiseshell products into many countries — the United States included — because the hawksbill turtle, from which the jewelry is made, is an endangered species. The center is open from 7:30 A.M. to 4:30 P.M. weekdays, although there is generally more activity in the morning.

NIGHTLIFE If you think a dive at Blue Corner is wild, try hitting some of the local bars in Koror, where a night on the town will leave you with plenty of stories to bring back home. Most of the bars have live bands that play songs by local artists to the beat of the ever-popular Palauan cha cha. Curfew is at midnight, but the sensible locals leave around 11:30, before the action in front of the bar moves to the hospital emergency room.

Fruit bats were once common throughout Micronesia, but the species has become threatened in recent years because of the popularity of fruit bat soup, especially in the Marianas. Fruit bat soup is also served in several restaurants in Palau where fruit bats are, for the time being, still common. However, it is much more enjoyable to see them soaring high above the Rock Islands than floating — head, wings and all — in a bowl of soup.

*P*alau is in the midst of an economic
boom. Hotels, large and small, are springing up throughout the islands. The
following are the few that were open for business at the time of publication. For
information on newer hotels, contact the Palau Visitors Authority, P.O. Box 256,
Koror, Palau 96940; phone (680) 488-2793; fax (680) 488-1453.

CARP ISLAND Carp Island Resort is a rustic, beach-front dive lodge located on the
island of Ngercheu. It's an hour's boat ride from Koror but only twenty minutes
from the popular dive sites in southern Palau. Though it has long been a favorite
with Japanese divers, other tourists are just now discovering it. The island itself
is gorgeous — shaded by coconut palm and ironwood trees, cooled by tropical
breezes and fronted by a meandering white sand beach. At low tide, you can join
the staff for a pick-up game of beach baseball or walk almost all the way around
the island exploring the many small, secluded coves. This pristine island is unspoiled and uninhabited save for the phantom spirit that reportedly wanders the
grounds at night making sure that all visitors are on their best behavior. Accommodations at the resort vary from spartan, dormitory-style cottages which share
communal showers to individual bungalows with private bathrooms. Meals are
typically Japanese and are served family style. Electricity to the cabins is turned
off at 10:00 P.M. so if you plan on some late-night reading, bring a battery-
powered light. Also bring mosquito repellent. For rates and reservations contact
Carp Corporation, P.O. Box 5, Koror, Palau 96940; phone (680) 488-2978, fax
(680) 488-1725.

*Carp Island Resort is located on the beautiful island of Ngercheu, just twenty minutes from
the popular dive sites in southern Palau.*

THE VILLAGE OF NGARAARD If you really want to get away from it all, the village of Ngaraard, an hour away from Koror by boat, has several traditional island-style resorts situated on an idyllic sand beach, the longest stretch of beach in Palau. Bring a book, your tired mind and an energy level that requires nothing more than lying in a hammock while listening to the waves crashing against the offshore reef. The beaches in this part of Palau are breathtaking. Miles of powdery white sand strewn with huge black boulders stretch up and down the coast as far as the eye can see. You can easily walk for more than two hours without meeting a single soul.

The Ngaraard Traditional Resort in the hamlet of Ulimang was the first and, for a long time, only resort in this part of Palau. This small, family-run operation rents three older-style cottages which can sleep from two to five people each. The resort is rustic. The generator runs only from 6:00 P.M. until midnight. There is no air-conditioning, but a steady onshore breeze generally cools the rooms. Bathroom and shower facilities are located in a separate building and there is no hot water. But the meals alone are worth the stay. Delicious local foods including mangrove crab, fresh fish and taro leaf soup are served in the beach-front bar. The bar itself is like a snapshot from the past — four-foot turtle shells hang from the inside walls which are strung with tattered fishing nets full of glass floats. A lonely pool table sits in the middle of the room and stacks of 45s and a lone Peter, Paul and Mary album lie on a shelf in a quiet corner. In addition to relaxing accommodations, the resort also offers tours (for its guests only) to the stone monoliths of Badrulchau and a hike to the Ngardmau Waterfall. There is also an extensive system of ancient stone paths just a ten-minute walk from the resort. These paths are not always maintained and are sometimes overgrown with grass but it is still worth the effort to see them. The main path takes you all the way to the center of an ancient village

With a balancing act only nature could perform, this enormous Rock Island defies the laws of gravity. Equally as impressive are the large trees that have managed to find a foothold in the solid limestone rock.

where you can see the weathered remains of old stone *bai* platforms. For rates and reservations contact the Ngaraard Traditional Resort, P.O. Box 773, Koror, Palau, 96940; phone (680) 488-1788; fax (680) 488-1725.

At the time of publication, a newer resort with island-style bungalows was under construction in the nearby hamlet of Chol. Check with the Palau Visitors Authority for the address and phone number. Also, the new road to Ngaraard was nearing completion so access to both resorts may be available by car.

THE STORYBOARD BEACH RESORT A new hotel with six thatch-roofed, beach-front cottages recently opened on the historic island of Peleliu. Combining traditional Palauan architecture with modern conveniences, each cottage has its own lanai, bathroom facilities and electricity during the evening hours. Accommodations are low key but charming and are ideal for both divers and nondivers alike, since the hotel is only a ten-minute boat ride from the famous Peleliu Wall or just minutes away from miles of empty, white sand beaches. Guided tours of Peleliu's caves, monuments and historic war relics can be arranged by the hotel staff along with snorkeling tours and local-style hand-line fishing excursions. And be sure to check out the local swimming hole, a sinkhole in the middle of the island whose water level rises and falls with the tide. At the time of publication, plans were under-way for an open-air restaurant serving breakfast, lunch and dinner, but before you go check with the hotel to find out whether or not meals are available. The hotel provides transportation to the island by boat or you can fly to Peleliu on Paradise Air. If you plan to fly to Peleliu with dive gear, be sure to check with the airline about luggage restrictions or contact the hotel and arrange to transport your dive equipment by boat. For more information, contact the Storyboard Beach Resort, P.O. Box 1561, Koror, Palau 96940; phone/fax (680) 488-3280.

This lovely flower, locally known as rur, *grows in the Rock Islands.*

HOTELS IN KOROR Hotel accommodations range from the luxurious Palau Pacific Resort, with private beach, landscaped gardens, swimming pool, tennis courts and health club, to the sparse but comfortable DW Motel, conveniently located in the center of town. Several popular medium-priced hotels, designed with the Western tourist in mind, include the Palau Marina Hotel, located on the water next to one of the well-known dive shops, and the Sunrise Villa, built on a quiet hillside with spectacular ocean views and a private swimming pool. The Hotel Nikko Palau, an older hotel built into a beautifully landscaped hillside, overlooks a serene cove of peaceful Rock Islands. And Palau's newest accommodations, The Carolines, offer upscale island-style bungalows, perched high on a hill with yet more gorgeous views of the Rock Islands. There are many additional hotels, ranging from economy to business class, located in the central business district. For further information contact the Palau Visitors Authority, Box 256, Koror, Palau, 96940; phone (680) 488-2793; fax (680) 488-1453. {PALAU PACIFIC RESORT, P.O. Box 308, Koror, Palau 96940; phone (680) 488-2600; fax (680) 488-1601. DW MOTEL, P.O. Box 738, Koror, Palau 96940; phone (680) 488-2641; fax (680) 488-1725. PALAU MARINA HOTEL, P.O. Box 142, Koror, Palau 96940; phone (680) 488-1786; fax (680) 488-1070. SUNRISE VILLA, P.O. Box 6009, Koror, Palau 96940; phone (680) 488-4590; fax (680) 488-4593. THE CAROLINES, P.O. Box 399, Koror, Palau 96940; phone (680) 488-1860; fax (680) 488-1858. HOTEL NIKKO PALAU, P.O. Box 310, Koror, Palau 96940; phone (680) 488-2486; fax (680) 488-2878}

DIVE OPERATORS There are a number of dive shops in Koror, but the following is a list of the largest shops, or the ones that cater to the English-speaking tourist. For a list of additional dive operators and companies specializing in land tours, contact the Palau Visitors Authority.

BELAU WATER SPORTS Specializes in all levels of PADI diving instruction courses for small groups of one to four with emphasis on environmental sensitivity towards marine life. Also offers diving and camping trips for small groups. Belau Water Sports, P.O. Box 680, Koror, Palau 96940; phone (680) 488-2349; fax (680) 488-1725.

FISH 'N FINS Full and half-day tours to all popular dive sites plus WWII wrecks. Snorkeling and night dives available on request. Dive shop located adjacent to the Palau Marina Hotel. NAUI instruction and rental equipment available. Fish 'n Fins, P.O. Box 142, Koror, Palau 96940; phone (680) 488-2637; fax (680) 488-1070.

NECO MARINE Full and half-day tours to all popular dive sites. Snorkeling and night dives available on request. Diving in Angaur available on request and weather permitting. Full service dive shop on premises sells dive equipment and wide selection of books on marine environment. PADI instruction and rental equipment available. Neco Marine, P.O. Box 129, Koror, Palau 96940; phone (680) 488-1755; fax (680) 488-2880.

PALAU DIVING ADVENTURES Full and half-day tours to all popular dive sites for small groups of six to eight divers. Snorkeling, WWII wrecks and night dives available on request. PADI instruction and rental equipment available. Palau Diving Adventures, P.O. Box 1714 #S-103, Koror, Palau 96940; phone/fax (680) 488-3548.

PALAU DIVING CENTER Full and half-day tours to all popular dive sites. Owns and operates Carp Island Resort, a dive hotel on a private rock island beach. Night diving and rental equipment available. NAUI and Japan Professional Divers Association instruction available. Palau Diving Center, P.O. Box 5, Koror, Palau 96940; phone (680) 488-2978; fax (680) 488-3155.

SAM'S DIVE TOURS Full and half-day tours for small groups to all popular dive sites. Specializes in dive sites off the beaten path as well as in Peleliu. WWII wrecks and night dives available on request. Also offers customized land tours to caves, waterfalls, historic war relics and monoliths. PADI instruction and rental equipment available. Sam's Dive Tours, P.O. Box 428, Koror, Palau 96940; phone (680) 488-1062; fax (680) 488-5003.

SPLASH Full and half-day tours for large and small groups to all the popular dive sites. Full service dive shop sells a wide selection of diving equipment and is located adjacent to the Palau Pacific Resort. PADI instruction and rental equipment available. Splash, P.O. Box 308, Koror, Palau 96940; phone (680) 488-2600; fax (680) 488-1601.

LIVEABOARD DIVE BOATS

OCEAN HUNTER Seven to ten-day cruises on board a 60-foot motor sailer offering unlimited diving to Palau's best-known sites as well as exploring uncharted reefs. Space limited to six divers in three air-conditioned cabins. See and Sea Travel, 50 Francisco St., Suite 205, San Francisco, CA 94133; phone 800-DIV-XPRT, (415) 434-3400; fax (415) 434-3409.

PALAU AGGRESSOR II Seven-day cruises to Palau's most popular dive sites aboard a luxury 100-ft power catamaran with a 30-ft. beam. Accommodations for 16 passengers in eight air-conditioned staterooms, each with private bath. Aggressor Fleet, P.O. Drawer K, Morgan City, LA 70381; phone 800-348-2628, (504) 385-2628; fax (504) 384-0817.

SUN DANCER Seven and ten-day dive cruises to Palau's most popular dive sites on board a luxury 16-passenger liveaboard with eight air-conditioned staterooms, each with private bath. The boat also runs trips to Palau's remote Southwest Islands. Peter Hughes Diving, 6851 Yumuri St., Suite 10, Coral Gables, FL 33146; phone 800-932-6237, (305) 669-9391; fax (305) 669-9475.

ENVIRONMENT

A Field Guide to the Birds of Hawaii and the Tropical Pacific, by H. Douglas Pratt, Phillip L. Bruner and Delwyn G. Barrett (Princeton University Press, 1987)

Field Guide to the Birds of Palau, by John Engbring (Prepared by the Conservation Office in cooperation with the Bureau of Education, Koror, Palau, 1988)

Field Guide to Anemonefishes and their Host Sea Anemones, by Daphne G. Fautin and Gerald R. Allen (Western Australian Museum, 1992)

Micronesian Reef Fishes, by Robert F. Myers (Coral Graphics, Box 21153, GMF, Barrigada, Guam 96921, second edition, 1991)

Ocean Life, Volume 2, Micronesia, a CD ROM (Sumeria, Inc., San Francisco, 1993)

Seven Underwater Wonders of the World, by Rick Sammon (Thomasson-Grant, Charlottesville, Virginia, 1992)

This Living Reef, by Douglas Faulkner (Quadrangle, New York Times Company, NY, 1974)

Words of the Lagoon, by R.E. Johannes (University of California Press, Berkeley, 1981)

GENERAL

A Reporter in Micronesia, by E.J. Kahn (W.W. Norton, New York, 1966)

A Song for Satawal, by Kenneth Brower (Penguin Books, New York, 1983)

Bai, by Marciana Telmetang, edited by Faustina K. Rehuher (Belau National Museum, Koror, Palau, 1993)

Micronesia: The Land, the People and the Sea, by Kenneth Brower (Louisiana State University Press, Baton Rouge, 1981)

Micronesian Customs and Beliefs, by the Students of the Community College of Micronesia, compiled and edited by Gene Ashby (Rainy Day Press, Eugene, Oregon, second edition, 1985)

Palau, Portrait of Paradise, by Mandy Etpison (Neco Marine Book Dept., Box 129, Koror, Palau 96940, 1993)

Palauan Social Structure, by DeVerne Reed Smith (Rutgers University Press, New Brunswick, New Jersey, 1983)

Prehistoric Architecture in Micronesia, by William N. Morgan (University of Texas Press, Austin, 1988)

The Edge of Paradise, America in Micronesia, by P.E. Kluge (Random House, NY, 1991)

With Their Islands Around Them, by Kenneth Brower (Holt, Rinehart and Winston, New York, 1974)

HISTORY

An Account of the Pelew Islands, by George Keate (1788). This extremely old volume is difficult to find and a joy to read. Try the rare book section of the library.

A History of Palau, Volumes I, II and III, edited by Katherine Kesolei (Palau Community Action Agency, Koror, Palau, 1976)

Lee Boo of Belau, A Prince in London, by Daniel J. Peacock (University of Hawaii Press, Honolulu, 1987)

Peleliu 1944, by Harry A. Gailey (Nautical and Aviation Publishing Company of America, Annapolis, Maryland, 1983)

Peleliu, Tragic Triumph, by Bill D. Ross (Random House, New York, 1991)

The First Taint of Civilization, by Francis X. Hezel, S.J. (University of Hawaii Press, Honolulu, 1983)

SHIPWRECKS

Desecrate One, The Shipwrecks of Palau, by Klaus Lindemann (Pacific Press Publications, Belleville, Michigan, 1989)

WW II Wrecks of Palau, by Dan E. Bailey (North Valley Diver Publications, Redding, California, 1991)

GUIDEBOOKS

Adventuring in the Pacific, The Sierra Club Travel Guide to the Islands of Polynesia, Melanesia and Micronesia, by Susanna Margolis (Sierra Club Books, San Francisco, revised edition, 1996)

Diving and Snorkeling Guide to Palau, by Tim Rock and Francis Toribiong (Pisces Books, A Division of Gulf Publishing Company, Houston, 1994)

Micronesia, A Travel Survival Kit, by Glenda Bendure and Ned Friary (Lonely Planet Publications, Victoria, Australia, second edition, 1992)

Micronesia Handbook: Guide to the Caroline, Gilbert, Mariana, and Marshall Islands, by David Stanley (Moon Publications, Chico, CA, third edition, 1992)

The Adventure Guide to Micronesia, by T. and V. Booth (Hunter Publishing, Edison, NJ, 1991)

KAYANGEL

19

P   A   C   I   F   I

P   H   I   L   I   P   P   I   N   E   S   E

Palau
Islands

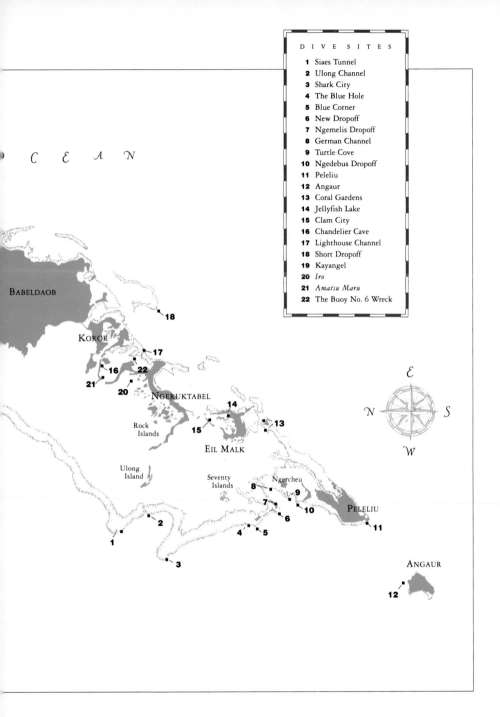

ACKNOWLEDGMENTS

I met many wonderful people in Palau without whose help this book would not have been possible. My sincere appreciation goes to Mandy and Shallum Etpison who generously offered their warm friendship and hospitality when I first came to Palau in 1986. I especially want to thank Mandy for inspiring me to write this book in the first place. ¶ Most of the diving information presented here is the result of countless conversations with many members of the local diving community. They are the true experts. For their help, I am grateful to the following people: Anna Fahlen, Johnny Kishigawa, Dennis Moros, Blanco Olsingch, Keith Santillano, Sam Scott, Bena Sukuma, Sam Whipps, and Sabah and Ray. My special thanks goes to Francis Toribiong and the staff at Fish 'n Fins: Winkler Maech, Lenny Oberg, Melvin Toribiong, Masao Udui, and the many others who were always willing to answer my questions. ¶ I am also indebted to a number of individuals for insights into the culture of Palau. P. Kempis Madd allowed me access to the Belau National Museum's priceless collection of books and patiently endured my many questions about the Palauan legends. Simeon Adelbai of the Museum staff related his beautiful version of the legend of Ulong and allowed me to use the historical photographs of Palau. Joshua Koshiba told me his family legend of the old woman of Ngercheu. And Norma Sumang explained the subtleties of the legends so that they retained their original Palauan meaning when rewritten for the Western reader. A heartfelt thanks also goes to Margo Vitarelli for her great ideas, support and friendship. She and Tina Rehuher of the Belau National Museum reviewed certain portions of the manuscript at the last minute and offered valuable suggestions. ¶ A number of people helped ensure the accuracy of the historical and scientific information. Ann and Clarence Kitalong critically reviewed sections of the manuscript. Dan Bailey helped write portions of the text on Palau's World War II shipwrecks, and Klaus Lindemann allowed me to use his illustrations. Gerry Heslinga always found time to answer my questions on giant clams. Larry Sharon generously offered information about Palau's marine lakes. Lisa King at the Marine Resources Division gave many appreciated suggestions. Noah Idechong offered his insights into the conservation efforts in Palau. And Chuck Cook and Dr. Marty Fujita provided useful information published by the Nature Conservancy in Palau. Any misinformation that appears in this book is my fault, not theirs. ¶ Working with a good editor is like having a partner who is as interested as the author in producing good work. With her demands for clarity, conciseness and the logical ordering of information, Elaine de Man's high standards ultimately resulted in a more polished manuscript. I thank her for always being there. ¶ A number of photographers contributed significantly to making the beauty of these islands come alive in the pages of this book: Kevin Davidson, Al Giddings, Murray Kaufman, Avi Klapfer, Neil Montanus, Hiroshi Nagano, Ed Robinson, Sam Sargent, Rick Tegeler, Mitchell P. Warner and Jan and Bert Yates. Thank you for your exquisite photographs of Palau. Any photographs that appear in this book without a credit were taken by the author. ¶ Most of the legends that appear in this book were found in a folder of loose pages stashed away in a quiet corner of the Belau Museum. A few, however, came from other sources. The legend about the girl who turned into a dugong was found in *Micronesian Customs and Beliefs,* written by the students of the Community College of Micronesia, compiled and edited by Gene Ashby, Rainy Day Press, 1985. The opening legend of Uchelianged was discovered in a brochure published by the Palau Pacific Resort. Additional proverbs were found in *Micronesian Research Working Papers,* collected and compiled by Robert K. McKnight with the help of Adalbert Obak and Erminia Ngiraked, edited by John E. de Young, published by the Office of the High Commissioner, Trust Territory of the Pacific Islands, 1966. I thank the publishers for making this information available. ¶ And finally, one can never overlook the value of friendship in an undertaking such as this, especially when working far from home. I am forever grateful to Cindy and Damien Fitzpatrick, Max and Kerkar Moros, and John and Jill McCready. I would also like to thank my family and friends at home who patiently tolerated my obsession with "the book" and my long periods of isolation, and Mark and Patty Rojec, Jim Senal, Tamera Gabel and John Babcock for their much needed support at the last minute. ¶ To all of you, and the many others who gave additional help, I offer my heartfelt appreciation.

Ed Robinson